Malta TRAVEL GUIDE 2023-2024

Unveiling Adventures, Culinary Delights, Rich History, and Cozy Accommodation

Alex Fowler

Copyright © by Alex Fowler 2023.

All rights reserved.

Except for brief quotations used in critical reviews and other non-commercial uses permitted by copyright law, no part of this publication may be copied, distributed, or transmitted in any way without the publisher's prior written consent, including by photocopying, recording, or other electronic or mechanical methods.

The use of any trademarks or brands mentioned in this book is solely for the purpose of clarification and is not intended to imply any affiliation with the respective owners of those marks or brands.

TABLE OF CONTENTS

INTRODUCTION

CHAPTER 1

History And Culture

   Geography and Climate

CHAPTER 2

Best Time to Visit

   Visa and Entry Requirements

   Travel Tips and Practical Information

   Language and Communication

   Local Customs and Etiquette

   Health and Safety

CHAPTER 3

How to Get There

Transportation Options

   Air Travel Options

   Ferry and cruise options

   Malta Map View

CHAPTER 4

Accommodation

   Luxury Hotels and Resorts

   Mid-Range Options

   Budget-Friendly Stays

Bed and Breakfasts
Self-Catering Apartments
CHAPTER 5
Must-Visit Places
Mdina - The Silent City
Gozo Island
Historical Sites
St. John's Co-Cathedral
Hagar Qim Temples
Natural Wonders
Blue Grotto
Dingli Cliffs
CHAPTER 6
Coastal Attractions
Marsaxlokk Fishing Village
Xlendi Bay
Marsalforn Bay
Sliema Promenade
CHAPTER 7
Restaurants and Cuisine
Maltese Cuisine
Popular Restaurants
Cafes
Ta' Kris

The Harbour Club
Noni
Street Food Delights
Food and Wine Festivals
CHAPTER 8
Itinerary Suggestions
   One Week Itinerary
   Cultural Exploration
   Relaxation and Beach Time
CHAPTER 9
Beaches
   Mellieha Bay
   Ramla Bay
   Paradise Bay
   Ghajn Tuffieha Bay
   Riviera Beach
CHAPTER 10
Outdoor Activities
   Water Sports and Diving
   Hiking and Nature Trails
   Boat Trips and Excursions
CHAPTER 11
Shopping In Malta

    Traditional Crafts and Souvenirs
    Local Markets and Shopping Districts
CHAPTER 12
Nightlife and Entertainment
    Music and Festivals
    Theater and Performing Arts
    Useful Malta Phrases
CONCLUSION

INTRODUCTION

Nestled among the glittering seas of the Mediterranean Sea, Malta is a fascinating island overflowing with history, culture, and natural grandeur. This little island country, frequently forgotten among its bigger European competitors, hides within a universe of delights waiting to be exposed by eager tourists.

Picture yourself wandering through the old alleys of Valletta, Malta's enchanting capital city, where great palaces and fortified walls remain as quiet sentinels of a brilliant past. Imagine experiencing the underground mysteries of Ħal Saflieni Hypogeum, a UNESCO World Heritage Site that has enthralled archaeologists and history fans for decades.

Delve into Malta's rich cultural fabric, where the echoes of past civilizations blend with the vivid customs of today. Witness the excitement of a typical Maltese Festa, when streets explode in a kaleidoscope of colors, music, and fireworks. Savor the tastes of traditional Maltese cuisine, a delightful blend of Mediterranean and North African influences.

Venture beyond the boundaries of Malta's main island and explore the serene beauty of Gozo and Comino, its sister islands. Hike along steep cliffs, bathe in crystal-clear waterways, and enjoy in the calm of pristine natural scenery.

Malta is an island that calls to the spirit, a place where history intertwines with the present, where culture pulsates with life, and where nature paints a stunning painting. It is a location that will leave you enthralled, your heart filled with memories that will last long after your departure. So, pack your bags, embrace the spirit of adventure, and go on a vacation to Malta, a Mediterranean treasure that promises an amazing experience.

CHAPTER 1

History And Culture

With its rich tapestry of civilizations, from the intriguing Megalithic Temple Builders to the brave Knights of St. John, Malta has a narrative to tell that spans millennia.

Stepping Back in Time: Malta's Enduring Legacy

Imagine standing before the towering megalithic temples of Malta, some of the oldest free-standing monuments in the world, their megaliths gently whispering stories of a civilization that existed almost 5,000 years ago. These UNESCO World Heritage Sites, such as the towering Tarxien Temples and the intriguing Ħal Saflieni Hypogeum, serve as testaments to the inventiveness and architectural talent of Malta's early inhabitants.

Knights of St. John: Guardians of Malta's Heritage

In the 16th century, the Knights of St. John, a gallant order of military monks, came to Malta, converting the island into a powerful stronghold. Valletta, Malta's capital city, is a living tribute to their heritage, with its massive defenses, majestic palaces, and exquisite churches. The Knights' influence penetrates Maltese culture, from the characteristic eight-pointed Maltese cross to the yearly Festas, exuberant events staged in honor of local saints.

A Fusion of Cultures: Malta's Tapestry of Traditions

Malta's history is a tapestry woven by many civilizations, each leaving its unmistakable stamp on the island's traditions and customs. Phoenicians, Romans, Arabs, Normans, and the British have all contributed to Malta's distinct cultural character. The Maltese language, a combination of Arabic and Sicilian, represents this rich linguistic past, while the island's food is a fascinating blend of Mediterranean tastes.

Feasts for the Senses: Malta's Culinary Delights
Maltese cuisine is a symphony of tastes, a delicious blend of Mediterranean and North African influences. Fresh local vegetables, fresh fish, and fragrant spices dance together on the palette, producing a gastronomic experience that is both genuine and memorable. Sample the savory pastizzi, a flaky pastry filled with ricotta or peas, or indulge in the substantial fenek, a rabbit stew that is a hallmark of Maltese cuisine.

Island Beauty: Malta's Natural Splendors
Malta's natural beauty is as appealing as its history and culture. The turquoise seas of the Mediterranean Sea lap against the island's rocky coasts, while the sun-drenched surroundings provide a kaleidoscope of hues and textures. Explore the secluded coves of Comino, dive in the crystal-clear seas of Gozo, or climb along the

majestic cliffs of Dingli, where the vistas reach eternally into the horizon.

Malta: A Cultural Mosaic Waiting to be Explored

Malta is a treasure mine of cultural experiences, ready to be found by the adventurous tourist. Immerse yourself in the vivid atmosphere of a typical Maltese Festa, when the streets come alive with music, dancing, and fireworks. Visit the Malta National Theatre, headquartered in the beautiful Manoel Theatre, and observe the island's booming cultural culture.

Malta is a location that will capture your senses, leaving you with a heart full of memories and a yearning to return. It is an island where history whispers in the breeze, where culture vibrates in every corner, and where natural beauty unfolds like a stunning picture. Come, experience Malta, and let its ageless charm weave its enchantment around you.

Geography and Climate

Malta's unique character and allure of the island are greatly influenced by its climate and geographical features.

Map of Malta's Geography

Malta is made up of three main inhabited islands, each with its unique charm: Comino, Gozo, and Malta. The largest island, Malta, is home to the vibrant capital city of Valletta and has a varied topography that includes quaint villages, rolling hills, and a gorgeous shoreline. Gozo, also referred to as the "sister island," has a serene aura thanks to its lush countryside, secluded bays, and historic ruins. The least populated island, Comino, is a nature lover's paradise with its isolated lagoon, pristine waters, and profusion of marine life.

Climate of the Mediterranean: A Harmony of Sun and Sea

Malta experiences mild, rainy winters and warm, dry summers typical of a Mediterranean climate. From June to August, the summer months are usually bright and warm, with average highs of 25°C to 32°C (77°F to 90°F). The sea entices with its cool waters, offering a much-needed break from the summer heat. Average temperatures during the moderate and rainy winter, which lasts from December to February, range from 12°C to 16°C (54°F to 61°F). Rainfall on the island averages 600 millimeters per year, with the majority of the precipitation falling during the winter.

The Influence of Climate and Geography on Malta's Allure

Malta's civilization, culture, and natural beauty have all been greatly influenced by its unique geography and climate. Throughout history, trade and navigation have been made easier by the untamed coastline and its deep bays and harbors. The island's culinary customs have been shaped by agriculture on the land that the fertile valleys and undulating hills have offered. The whitewashed dwellings and shaded streets of the island, which are intended to offer relief from the summer sun, are a result of the island's Mediterranean environment.

Discovering the Geographical Jewels of Malta

The geographical diversity of Malta presents a multitude of chances for exploration. Take in the expansive vistas from the Dingli Cliffs, explore the catacombs of Rabat, or tour the ancient temples of Ħal Saflieni Hypogeum in Paola. Discover the Citadel in Victoria, Gozo; take a stroll through the bucolic Comino landscapes; or see the Blue Lagoon, an untouched natural wonder.

Adopting the Mediterranean Climate of Malta

Malta's weather is ideal for outdoor recreation and dining al fresco. Take leisurely walks along Sliema's promenade, bask in the sun on Golden Bay's beaches, or go trekking and biking in the surrounding countryside. Experience the flavors of

Maltese cuisine at authentic eateries where the focus is on fresh seafood and regional specialties.

Allow Malta's varied terrain and temperate climate to lead the way as you tour the island. Experience the island's dynamic culture, which has been influenced by its distinctive geographical tapestry and Mediterranean allure, as you explore ancient ruins surrounded by breathtaking scenery, and bask in the warmth of the sun and the cool sea breeze.

CHAPTER 2

Best Time to Visit

While Malta's attractiveness continues throughout the year, there are specific seasons that provide an especially lovely experience for guests.

Sunshine and Warmth: The Allure of Summer (June-August)

For those seeking sun-kissed days and pleasant nights, summer in Malta is the perfect season to come. The Mediterranean sunbeams abundantly, pouring its warm warmth across beaches, towns, and ancient landmarks. The sea invites with its welcoming waves, suitable for swimming, snorkeling, and diving.

Shoulder Seasons: A Balance of Charm and Serenity (April-May, September-October)

If you prefer a warmer temperature and fewer people, the shoulder seasons of spring and fall provide a lovely alternative to the prime summer months. The weather continues delightfully warm, with temperatures ranging from the mid-20s to the mid-30s Celsius. The throngs clear down, allowing for a more calm and tranquil tour of the island.

Mellow Winters: Unveiling Malta's Tranquil Side (November-March)

While the winter months bring milder temperatures, Malta still basks in an average of 15 degrees Celsius, making it a lovely option for visitors seeking a calm retreat. The crowds lessen further, allowing a tranquil environment to explore the island's historical riches and natural beauties.

Festive Splendor: A Special Time to Visit

Malta's calendar is peppered with vivid festivals throughout the year, giving an added layer of excitement to your stay. The Feast of St. Peter and St. Paul in June is a national event, while the Malta

International Arts Festival in July exhibits the island's cultural skills. The Christmas season turns Malta into a paradise of lights and celebrations.

Choosing Your Perfect Malta Adventure

The ideal time to visit Malta ultimately relies on your unique choices and goals. If you desire sun-soaked days and boisterous atmospheres, summer is your excellent option. For a combination of great weather and fewer people, the shoulder seasons provide a lovely respite. And if you desire a calm experience with a touch of festive flair, winter might be a beautiful season to come.

Regardless of when you choose to go on your Maltese trip, the island promises to uncover its secrets, leaving you with a heart full of memories and a wish to return.

Visa and Entry Requirements

While visa requirements for Malta differ based on your country, knowing the procedure assures a smooth and seamless admission into this enchanting island location.

Visa-Exempt Countries for Malta

If you are a citizen of any of the following countries, you do not need to get a visa to visit Malta for a stay of up to 90 days during 180 days:

European Union (EU) member states
- Schengen Agreement member states

- Other chosen nations, including the United States, Canada, Australia, New Zealand, and Japan

Obtaining a Visa for Malta

If you are not a citizen of a visa-exempt nation, you will need to get a visa to visit Malta. The sort of visa you require depends on your purpose of travel and the duration of your stay. Here are the major kinds of visas available:

- Short-stay visa (Schengen visa): This visa is valid for up to 90 days within 180 days and is designed for tourists and business visitors.

- Long-stay visa: This visa is valid for a longer duration, often up to one year, and is designed for persons who want to study, work, or remain in Malta for a prolonged period.

Application Process for a Malta Visa

To apply for a Malta visa, you will need to provide the following documents:
- A completed visa application form

- Two recent passport-sized photographs

- Your valid passport with at least six months of validity remaining

Proof of travel insurance
- Proof of adequate financial resources to maintain yourself throughout your stay

- Other supporting papers depending on the kind of visa you are asking for

Applying for a Visa in Advance

It is strongly suggested to apply for your Malta visa well in advance of your intended trip date since processing periods might vary based on your nationality and the kind of visa you are requesting. You may apply for a visa at the closest Maltese embassy or consulate in your native country.

Entry Requirements for Malta

In addition to a visa, you will additionally need to satisfy the following entry criteria while visiting Malta:

- A valid passport with at least three months of validity remaining

- Onward or return ticket

- Proof of adequate financial resources to maintain yourself throughout your stay

Accommodation arrangements
- A completed passenger locator form (PLF) if coming from a red or heavy red list country

Additional Considerations
- Keep your passport and visa secure at all times.

- Be mindful of local laws and customs.

- Respect the Maltese people and culture.

- Enjoy your Maltese adventure responsibly.

Malta greets you with wide arms, eager to expose its riches and create memorable moments. By knowing the visa and entrance formalities, you can ensure a smooth and comfortable vacation to this wonderful island paradise.

Travel Tips and Practical Information

To guarantee a flawless and delightful visit, here's a reference to practical travel advice and information for your Maltese vacation.

Language and Communication:
Maltese is the official language, along with English. English is commonly spoken, especially in tourist regions, making conversation straightforward for most tourists.

Currency and Exchange Rates:
Malta's currency is the euro (€). ATMs are freely accessible around the island, and major payment cards are generally accepted.

Transportation:
Malta boasts a comfortable public transit system, consisting of buses and ferries. Buses link major cities and villages, while ferries carry people between Malta, Gozo, and Comino. Car rentals are

also available for individuals wanting extra freedom.

Accommodation:

Malta provides a varied choice of lodging alternatives, appealing to every budget and desire. From opulent hotels and lovely guesthouses to contemporary flats and historic farmhouses, you're sure to discover a great match.

Dining:

Maltese cuisine is a delicious combination of Mediterranean and North African influences, incorporating fresh local vegetables, caught fish, and fragrant spices. Sample classic pastizzi, relish fenek, a savoury rabbit stew, or indulge in Lampuki Pie, a flaky pastry stuffed with fish.

Shopping:

Malta provides a range of shopping experiences, from traditional souvenir stores to fashionable boutiques. Explore Valletta's busy retail alleys, peruse the artisan markets of Mdina, or discover local crafts and delights at the Malta Farmers' Market.

Nightlife:
Malta's nightlife culture provides something for everyone, from bustling pubs and clubs to traditional Maltese music venues and laid-back wine bars. Enjoy the exciting atmosphere of Paceville, St. Julian's entertainment area, or chill in the picturesque ambiance of Valletta's waterfront bars.

Practical Tips:
- Pack for warm conditions, particularly during summer months.
- Bring appropriate shoes for touring historical places and negotiating cobblestone alleys.
- Consider obtaining a multi-day bus ticket for easy mobility.

- Learn a few simple Maltese phrases to boost your contacts with locals.
- Respect local norms and traditions, particularly during religious holidays and celebrations.

Language and Communication

While English is frequently spoken in tourist areas, immersing oneself in the indigenous language, Maltese, may improve your travel experience and develop deeper ties with the island's population.

Maltese: A Language Steeped in History

Maltese, a Semitic language with Arabic origins, is a remarkable combination of linguistic elements, reflecting the island's rich history and complex cultural tapestry. While Italian and English have also contributed to its lexicon, Maltese preserves its own character, serving as a sign of national pride and cultural history.

English: A Gateway to Communication

English is commonly spoken in Malta, notably in tourist regions and service sectors. This extensive usage of English makes it easier for tourists to converse successfully throughout their stay. Whether seeking directions, ordering meals, or making queries, English offers a trustworthy bridge between tourists and residents.

Learning Basic Maltese Phrases: A Touch of Local Charm

While English is widely accessible, learning a few simple Maltese words may add a bit of local character to your interactions and display your respect for the island's past. Here are a few fundamental words to get you started:

- **Hello:** Bonġu (pronounced bon-joo)
- **Goodbye:** Adieu (pronounced ah-dyoo)
- **Thank you:** Grazzi (pronounced graht-zee)
- **You're welcome:** M'hemmx għalfejn (pronounced mm-hemx gal-fen)
- **Please:** Jekk jogħġbok (pronounced yek yo-gh-blok)
- **Do you speak English?:** Titkellem bl-Ingliż? (pronounced tit-kel-lem bl-ing-leez)

Non-Verbal Communication: Understanding Maltese Customs

Beyond spoken language, non-verbal communication plays an important part in Maltese culture. A nice grin, a warm handshake, and direct eye contact express respect and admiration. Patience and understanding are also needed, since natives may take their time during interactions.

Embracing the Linguistic Diversity of Malta

Malta's linguistic environment is a monument to its rich history and numerous cultural influences. While English serves as a handy medium for communication, adopting even a few simple Maltese words may enrich your trip experience, expand your awareness of the island's culture, and develop important ties with the local people. So, open your mind, accept the linguistic variety of Malta, and let the island's distinctive character enchant you.

Local Customs and Etiquette

Beyond its breathtaking scenery and historical riches, Malta provides a complex tapestry of customs and traditions that represent its distinct cultural history. To improve your Maltese journey, here's a guide on local customs and etiquette, helping you traverse the island's social terrain with elegance and respect.

Greetings and Interactions:

Maltese people are noted for their friendliness and kindness. Greetings are generally accompanied by a handshake or a warm grin. When addressing someone, use their title (Mr., Mrs., Ms.) followed by their surname. Direct eye contact and a genuine grin express respect and interest in the discourse.

Dining Etiquette:

Meals are generally a social occasion, enjoyed with family and friends. Table etiquette is usually informal, with the usage of utensils and chopsticks

35

being prevalent. When eating out, tipping is usual, often 10% of the cost.

Public Etiquette:
Respect for public areas and other persons is highly valued in Malta. Avoid trash, loud sounds, and impolite conduct. Dress modestly when visiting religious sites or attending cultural events. Smoking is forbidden in most public interior places and specified areas exclusively in outdoor venues.

Religious Observance:
Malta is a largely Catholic nation, and religious rituals play a big part in the everyday life of many inhabitants. Respectful dress is advised while visiting churches and religious organizations. During religious services, keep a calm and reverent approach.

Local Traditions and Celebrations:
Malta's cultural calendar is overflowing with exciting festivals and festivities. Immerse yourself

in the local spirit by attending a traditional Maltese Festa, a lively street party honoring a patron saint. During religious processions, offer adequate room for participants and keep a respectful distance.

Appreciation and Gratitude:

Expressing thanks is highly prized in Maltese society. Thanking your hosts, servers, and service providers with a heartfelt "Grazzi" (thank you) displays your gratitude for their hospitality. A tiny sign of thanks, such as a gift or memento, might also be a meaningful gesture.

Respecting Cultural Heritage:

Malta's rich cultural legacy is visible in its historical landmarks, archaeological riches, and traditional crafts. Treat these antiques and monuments with care, without touching or destroying them. When visiting museums or historical places, adhere to any specified norms or limits.

Embracing Cultural Sensitivity:

Malta, like every civilization, has its distinct customs and traditions. Approach cultural differences with an open mind and a readiness to learn. Avoid making assumptions or inappropriate statements, and instead, endeavor to learn and appreciate the island's cultural tapestry.

Remember, cultural etiquette is not about hard rules but about displaying respect and awareness for the customs and traditions of the country you are visiting. By embracing Malta's cultural subtleties, you'll enrich your vacation experience, form significant relationships, and create lasting memories of your Maltese adventure.

Currency and Banking

As you begin your Maltese trip, knowing the local currency and banking system will guarantee a seamless and happy encounter. This thorough book will provide you with the needed information to navigate the financial environment of Malta with confidence.

Currency Basics: Demystifying the Euro

Malta formally accepted the euro (€) in 2008, entering the eurozone with 18 other European states. The euro is divisible into 100 cents, and coins exist in denominations of 1, 2, 5, 10, 20, and 50 cents, €1, and €2. Euro banknotes are available in denominations of €5, €10, €20, €50, €100, €200, and €500.

Exchanging Your Currency: Turning Your Cash into Euros

Before stepping foot in Malta, you'll likely need to convert your local money for euros. You may accomplish this at several sites, including:

- **Banks:** Banks provide currency exchange services, although their prices may vary. Check with your bank beforehand to get the current exchange rate.

- **Currency Exchange Bureaus:** Dedicated currency exchange bureaus are generally accessible in tourist locations and offer competitive conversion rates.

- **Hotels:** While handy, hotels sometimes provide less advantageous exchange rates than banks or bureaus.

ATMs and Debit Cards: Convenient Cash Access

ATMs (Automated Teller Machines) are common in Malta, enabling you to withdraw euros straight from your bank account using your debit or credit card. However, most ATMs charge a transaction fee, so it's recommended to withdraw greater sums less often.

Credit Cards: A Widely Accepted Payment Option

Credit cards are commonly accepted in Malta for both in-store purchases and online transactions. Major credit card brands including Visa, Mastercard, and American Express are frequently accepted. Inform your bank about your trip intentions to prevent card freeze due to unexpected activity.

Travelers Cheques: A Less Common Option

Traveler's checks are still accepted in Malta, however, their use has fallen with the predominance of ATMs and credit cards. Check with your bank or currency exchange bureaus for availability and exchange rates.

Tipping Etiquette: A Gesture of Appreciation

While tipping is not necessary in Malta, it is traditional and appreciated, particularly for outstanding service in restaurants, hotels, and taxis. A small sum, such as 5-10% of the bill or a rounded-up number, is generally adequate.

Additional Tips for Financial Prudence

1. Notify Your Bank: Inform your bank of your trip intentions to prevent card freeze due to unexpected activity.

2. Protect Your Valuables: Keep your cash and valuables, such as passports and credit cards, in a secure area, such as a hotel safe or money belt.

3. Be Aware of Surroundings: Exercise care in busy settings and avoid exhibiting big sums of cash.

4. Carry Small Denominations: Having lower euro denominations ready is important for everyday shopping and gratuities.

5. Compare currency Rates: Check currency rates at several places to obtain the best discounts.

6. Use ATMs Strategically: Withdraw greater amounts less often to reduce transaction costs.

7. Retain Receipts: Keep receipts for all transactions to monitor spending and assist claims in case of anomalies.

8. Seek Assistance When Needed: Don't hesitate to contact bank officials or hotel workers if you have any inquiries or concerns.

Embrace your Maltese journey with financial certainty and experience the island's rich cultural history, spectacular natural beauty, and kind hospitality.

Health and Safety

Malta, an archipelago of beautiful islands set among the blue seas of the Mediterranean Sea, is recognized for its rich history, lively culture, and magnificent scenery. While Malta is a typically secure place for vacationers, it's always good to take steps to guarantee a healthy and worry-free holiday. Here's a complete guide to health and safety in Malta for tourists:

General Health and Safety Tips
- **Stay hydrated:** Malta's bright weather may contribute to dehydration, so it's vital to drink lots of water throughout the day. Carry a reusable water bottle and refill it frequently.

- **Protect yourself from the sun:** Malta's sun may be harsh, particularly during the summer months. Use sunscreen with a high SPF, wear a wide-brimmed hat, and seek shade during the warmest hours of the day.

44

- **Be careful of local customs and traditions:** Respect the local culture and dress properly for religious places and conservative regions.

- **Be careful with valuables:** Keep a tight check on your valuables, particularly in busy locations like public transit. Avoid bringing significant sums of cash or valuables with you.

- **Seek medical care if needed:** Malta's healthcare system is well-equipped to meet emergency and regular medical requirements. Don't hesitate to seek medical treatment if you feel sick or have an accident.

Specific Health Considerations
- **Vaccinations:** While no obligatory vaccinations are needed for travel to Malta,

it's advisable to consult with your doctor about any essential immunizations, particularly if you're going to participate in outdoor activities or contact with animals.

- **Mosquitoes:** Mosquitoes may be found in specific regions, especially during warmer months. Use insect repellent and wear long sleeves and trousers in the evenings to limit the chance of mosquito bites.

- **Food and water safety:** Malta's food and water are typically safe for eating. However, it's suggested to avoid tap water in rural regions and stick to bottled water. Choose trustworthy eateries and avoid ingesting raw fish if you have any worries.

Safety in Specific Situations

- **Swimming:** Malta's coastline provides various beaches and swimming possibilities. Always swim in authorized locations under the supervision of lifeguards. Be aware of strong currents and avoid swimming in stormy seas.

- **Hiking and outdoor activities:** Malta's landscape provides wonderful hiking paths and outdoor sports. Plan your trip carefully, wear suitable footwear, and alert someone of your location before starting out.

- **Driving:** Malta's roadways are typically well-maintained, however, traffic may be congested in metropolitan areas. Drive conservatively, respect traffic restrictions, and be mindful of local driving practices.

Emergency Contact Information
- **Police:** 112

- **Ambulance:** 119

- **Fire Department:** 112

Additional Tips for a Safe and Enjoyable Trip to Malta

- **Learn a few fundamental Maltese phrases:** Learning a few simple Maltese terms and phrases will boost your interactions with locals and make your vacation more pleasurable.

- **Be careful of local money and exchange rates:** Malta uses the euro (€) as its currency. Familiarize yourself with the exchange rates and bring adequate cash for your requirements.

- **Respect the environment:** Malta is devoted to environmental sustainability. Dispose of rubbish appropriately, prevent littering, and maintain the natural beauty of the islands.

- **Embrace the local culture:** Immerse yourself in Maltese culture by visiting museums, attending local events, and trying traditional food.

- **Create treasured memories:** Capture images, chronicle your experiences, and appreciate the distinctive environment of Malta to create lasting recollections of your visit.

CHAPTER 3

How to Get There

Whether you're seeking a speedy shuttle from the airport, a gorgeous boat trip, or the freedom of a hired automobile, Malta accommodates every travel type.

By Air:
Malta International Airport (MLA) is the principal entrance to the island, functioning as a hub for both local and international aircraft. Numerous airlines provide direct connections from major European cities, as well as links from farther afield. Once at the airport, you may easily reach your location by taxi, vehicle rental, or public transportation.

By Sea:
Ferries offer a handy and picturesque alternative to plane travel. Regular ferry services run between Malta and mainland Italy, Sicily, and other

Mediterranean locations. These ships provide a pleasant and peaceful voyage, enabling you to appreciate the panoramic views of the glittering sea.

Planning Your Arrival:

Upon arrival, whether by air or sea, you'll discover a selection of transportation alternatives to meet your requirements. Taxis are widely accessible at the airport and ferry terminals, allowing a quick and direct connection to your hotel. Car rentals are also available, offering the option to explore the island at your own speed. Public buses provide a cost-effective and extensive network, linking major cities and villages.

Essential Tips:

- Consider currency exchange alternatives before or upon arrival.

- Familiarize yourself with local transit alternatives and plan your route accordingly.

- Embrace the Maltese attitude of hospitality and enjoy the journey!

Transportation Options

Once you've settled into your hotel, consider these transit alternatives to see Malta's different landscapes and attractions:

- **Public Buses:** Malta's public bus network is broad and efficient, linking major cities, villages, and important tourist locations. With reasonable prices and a thorough route map, buses provide a quick and cost-effective method to explore the island.

- **Car Rentals:** Renting a vehicle gives you the maximum independence and flexibility to explore Malta at your speed. Venture beyond the usual route, find secret coves and make amazing moments as you traverse the island's picturesque roadways.

- **Taxis:** Taxis are commonly accessible in large cities and tourist locations, giving a handy and comfortable choice for shorter journeys or evening excursions. Agree on a fee with the taxi driver ahead to minimize surprises.

- **Walking and Cycling:** Malta's modest size and picturesque streets make it a lovely spot to explore on foot or by bicycle. Stroll along the seaside promenades, meander through small cobblestone alleyways, and find hidden jewels at your own slow pace.

- **Hop-On Hop-Off Buses:** For a full tour of Malta's attractions, try hop-on hop-off buses. These tour buses follow set routes, enabling you to jump off at your selected sites, explore at your speed, and then hop back on to resume your adventure.

Additional Tips:
- **Download a navigation app:** Familiarize yourself with the island's roads and sights by downloading a navigation app.

Embrace the daring spirit: Malta provides unusual transportation choices, such as traditional Maltese boats (luzzus) and horse-drawn carriages. Consider these choices for an unforgettable encounter

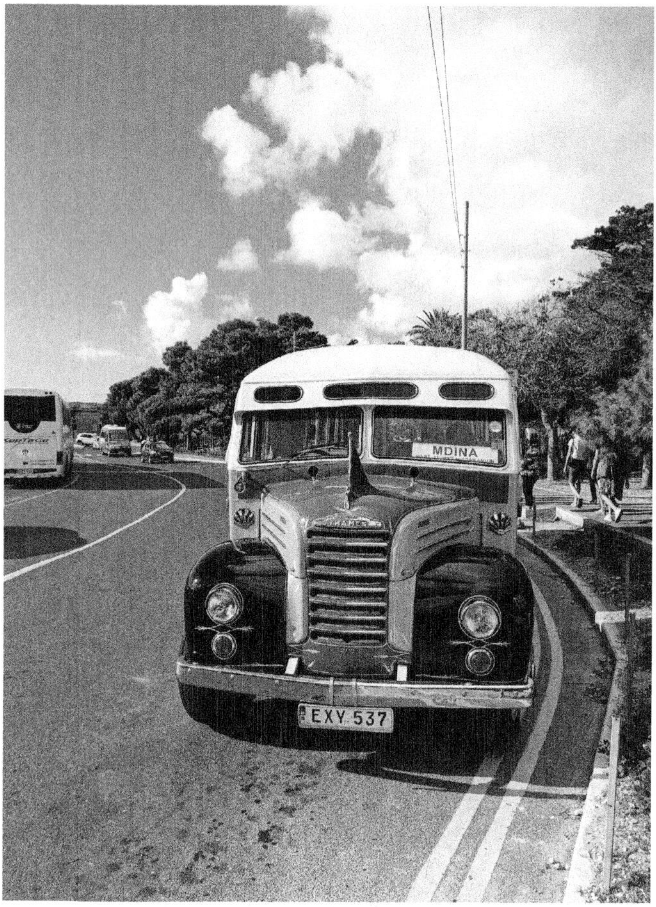
MDINA
EXY 537

Air Travel Options

Your Maltese Journey Begins at Malta International Airport (MLA) which is located in the center of the island, and serves as the major entrance to this enchanting location. Numerous airlines provide direct connections from major European cities, as well as links from farther afield. The airport features contemporary facilities, a variety of services, and efficient operations, assuring a pleasant and hassle-free arrival.

Navigating the Airport with Ease

Upon arrival at Malta International Airport, you'll discover a range of simple alternatives to navigate your surroundings and reach your preferred destination:

- **Taxis:** Taxi stands are widely accessible outside the airport terminals, allowing direct rides to hotels, lodgings, and other sites around the island.

- **Car Rentals:** For increased freedom and independence, automobile rental firms operate at the airport. Choose from a range of automobiles to meet your requirements and budget.

- **Public Buses:** Malta's vast public bus network links the airport to major cities and villages, giving a cost-effective and dependable alternative. Buses run often, giving a handy option to reach your location.

- **Hotel Shuttles:** Many hotels and resorts provide shuttle services from the airport to their own properties. Check with your lodging provider for availability and schedule.

Essential Tips for a Smooth Air Travel Experience

To guarantee a flawless and comfortable air travel experience, consider these vital tips:

1. Book your flights in advance: Especially during high season (June-August), reserving your flights in advance assures availability and typically obtains lower pricing.

2. Check visa requirements: Depending on your nationality, you may need a visa to enter Malta. Check visa requirements far ahead of your trip dates.

3. Familiarize yourself with luggage allowance regulations: Each airline has various luggage allowance requirements. Check your airline's luggage rules to avoid extra baggage costs.

4. Arrive at the airport with extra time: Allow sufficient time for check-in, security procedures, and probable delays. Aim to be at the airport at least two hours before your planned departure time.

As you begin your Maltese vacation, embrace the island's warm welcome and enjoy the voyage. Whether you're flying through the sky, navigating the airport, or discovering the island's riches, Malta awaits with open arms, eager to uncover its hidden jewels and create memorable experiences. Bon journey!

Ferry and cruise options

Malta's two major ferry ports, the Cirkewwa Ferry Terminal in the north and the Grand Harbour Ferry Terminal in Valletta serve as gates to the island.

These ports handle a range of ferry services, linking Malta to mainland Italy, Sicily, and other Mediterranean locations.

Ferry Options:

- **Standard Ferries:** Standard ferries provide a pleasant and dependable choice, with adequate seats and basic facilities. Travel duration spans from around 1.5 hours to 4.5 hours, depending on the location.

- **High-Speed Ferries:** For those wanting a speedier voyage, high-speed boats provide a quicker option, decreasing travel time by nearly half. These ships sometimes include extra facilities and services, such as on-board eateries and entertainment alternatives.

Booking Your Ferry Tickets:

To guarantee a pleasant and stress-free travel experience, it's advised to reserve your ferry tickets in advance, particularly during peak season (June-August). Online booking systems and ferry operator websites provide easy solutions for acquiring your tickets.

Upon Arrival at the Ferry Terminal:
Upon arriving at the ferry port, leave adequate time for check-in procedures and security inspections. Familiarize yourself with the boat timetable and boarding gate information. Once on board, sink into your seat, enjoy the panoramic views, and absorb the calm of the sea ride.

Exploring Malta's Coastline:
Sea travel provides the chance to experience Malta's shoreline from a unique viewpoint. Take in the scenery of the island's craggy cliffs, lovely towns

hidden around the shore, and the vivid hues of the Grand Harbour as you reach Valletta.

Additional Tips for a Pleasant Sea Travel Experience:

1. Check boat timetables and book in advance: Planning your travel and reserving tickets in advance assures a pleasant experience and prevents last-minute headaches.

2. Arrive at the ferry port with extra time: Allow sufficient time for check-in processes, security checks, and any delays.

3. Consider motion sickness treatments: If prone to motion sickness, see your doctor or pharmacist about suitable medicines.

4. Enjoy the sea wind and panoramic views: Embrace the peace of the sea voyage, relax, and take in the beauty of the Mediterranean countryside.

5. Embark on a day trip to Gozo or Comino: Seize the chance to take a day excursion to Gozo or Comino, sister islands of Malta, from the Cirkewwa port.

As you begin on your maritime journey, enjoy the peacefulness of the Mediterranean, relish the anticipation of reaching Malta's beaches, and prepare to be charmed by the island's rich legacy, captivating culture, and spectacular natural beauty. Bon journey!

Public Transport

To truly immerse yourself in the island's charm and explore its hidden jewels, Malta's public transit system provides a dependable and easy option to traverse your Maltese experience.

Malta's Public Bus Network: Your Gateway to Exploration

Malta's wide public bus network, run by Tallinja, links major cities, villages, and famous tourist locations, making it a perfect alternative for touring the island at your own speed. With reasonable rates and a thorough route map, the bus system provides a hassle-free and budget-friendly method to go about.

Purchasing Tickets and Planning Your Journey

To use the public bus system, consider acquiring a Tallinja Card, available in several forms, from single-day passes to multi-day and weekly choices. These cards provide cheaper rates and may be acquired at different sites, including airports, bus terminals, and approved stores.

Planning your bus travel is easy with the Tallinja App, available for iOS and Android smartphones. The app features real-time bus timetables, route maps, and travel planning tools, assuring you reach your location with ease.

Navigating the Bus System:
Upon arriving at your bus stop, examine the bus stop signs for information on routes, timetables, and stops. Boarding the bus, confirm your Tallinja Card using the specified card reader. Buses run routinely throughout the day, with increasing frequency during peak hours.

Exploring Malta's Enchanting Corners:
With its wide network, Malta's public bus system enables you to explore beyond the main route and discover the island's hidden secrets. From picturesque communities tucked in rolling hills to isolated coves along the coastline, the bus system gives access to a range of experiences.

Additional Tips for a Smooth Public Transportation Experience:

- **Familiarize oneself with the bus network:** Download the Tallinja App and examine the route map to plan your travels properly.

- **Consider local transit at peak hour:** Public buses may be busy during rush hour (between 7 am and 9 am, and 4 pm and 7 pm), so plan your travels appropriately.

- **Respect local traffic restrictions:** Always follow traffic laws and regulations to guarantee a safe and pleasurable experience for everybody.

- **Embrace the Maltese spirit of hospitality:** Engage with other passengers and locals, who are typically ready to offer their expertise and advice.

As you begin on your Maltese trip, let the public bus system lead you across the island's stunning landscapes and hidden jewels. With its ease, affordability, and accessibility, Malta's public transportation system offers a flawless and delightful trip, enabling you to completely immerse yourself in the island's rich past, lively culture, and spectacular natural beauty. Bon journey!

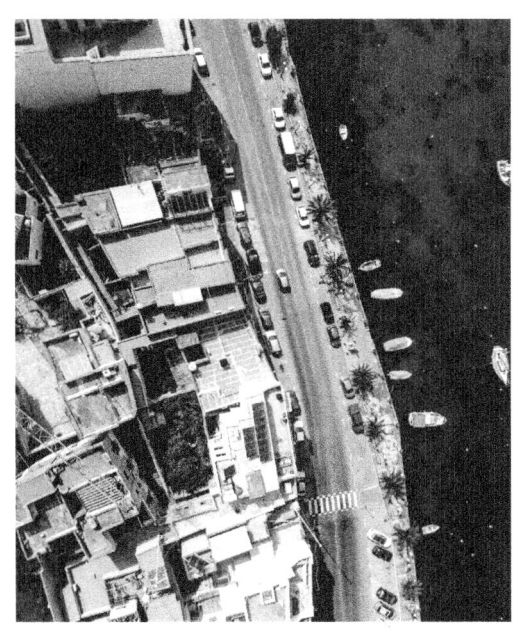

Rental Cars

While public transit is a convenient and cost-effective method to tour the island, renting a vehicle affords the greatest freedom and flexibility to wander beyond the main route and discover Malta's hidden jewels at your own speed.

Benefits of Renting a Car in Malta:
- **Unveiling Hidden Gems:** Car rentals open doors to Malta's lesser-known jewels, enabling you to discover hidden bays, quaint towns, and gorgeous landscapes that are typically unreachable by public transit.

- **Flexible Exploration:** With a rental vehicle, you're the boss of your agenda. Set your own speed, change your itinerary as you like, and relish the freedom to stop and explore whenever the need strikes.

- **Personalized Adventures:** Car rentals permit you to adapt your Maltese journey to your preferences. Whether you're seeking sun-drenched beaches, historic ruins, or bustling festivals, a rental vehicle puts the island's riches at your fingertips.

Renting a Car in Malta: Essential Tips and Procedures:

- **Planning Ahead:** Secure your automobile rental in advance, particularly during peak season (June-August), to assure availability and prevent last-minute headaches. Numerous international and local automobile rental businesses operate in Malta, providing a selection of cars to meet your demands and budget.

- **Essential Documentation:** Upon arriving at the automobile rental office, you'll need to provide your valid driver's license, passport, and confirmation of your booking. Additional documentation, such as an international driving permit, may be needed depending on your country.

- **Understanding Rental Terms and Conditions:** Carefully check the rental agreement before signing, ensuring you understand the terms and conditions, including insurance coverage, fuel regulations, and mileage limitations.

- **Navigating Malta's Roads:** Malta's roadways are typically well-maintained and simple to maneuver. Familiarize yourself with traffic laws and regulations, and consider utilizing navigation software like Google Maps or Waze to prevent getting lost.

Making the Most of Your Car Rental Adventure:
- Venture Beyond the Tourist Trail: Embrace Malta's variety by discovering lesser-known sites. Drive along meandering coastal roads, find secret coves, and immerse yourself in the original Maltese landscape.

- **Explore Malta's Diverse Landscapes:** From the craggy cliffs of Dingli to the peaceful beaches of Gozo, Malta's landscapes are as different as they are appealing. A rental automobile helps you to smoothly navigate between these various terrains.

- **Experience Malta's Festivals & Events:** Time your automobile rental to coincide with local festivals and events, such as the Malta Fireworks Festival or the Festa Sant'Antnin. Immerse yourself in the colorful Maltese culture and have amazing moments.

Additional Tips for an Enjoyable Car Rental Experience:

- **Plan your route in advance:** Utilize navigation tools to plan your travels properly, enabling you to optimize your time and avoid needless diversions.

- **Allow sufficient time for parking:** Parking places in big cities and tourist destinations might be restricted. Allow additional time in your schedule to locate parking and minimize tension.

- **Respect local traffic regulations:** Always follow to speed limits, traffic signs, and driving etiquette to ensure a safe and pleasurable experience for yourself and others.

- **Admire the Maltese scenery:** Take time to absorb the beauty of Malta's countryside while you drive. Stop at stunning views, grab amazing images, and experience the calm of the island's natural grandeur.

With its ease, flexibility, and capacity to discover hidden gems, renting a vehicle in Malta provides an unequaled chance to explore the island's breathtaking beauty and have amazing experiences. Embrace the freedom of the open road, immerse yourself in the real Maltese atmosphere, and explore the island's hidden beauties at your own leisure. Bon journey!

Taxis and Ride-Sharing

While public transit and auto rentals give handy choices for visiting the island, taxis and ride-sharing services provide an alternate method to discover Malta's picturesque streets and hidden jewels.

Taxis: A Convenient and Comfortable Option

Taxis are easily accessible in major cities and tourist locations, enabling a comfortable and direct journey to your intended destination. Taxi stands are instantly recognized by their characteristic yellow hue and are positioned at strategic spots around the island, including airports, ferry terminals, important tourist sites, and hotels.

Booking a Taxi:

Calling a cab is a basic affair. You may either hail a cab from the street or call a taxi company directly. Numerous taxi firms operate in Malta, and many have mobile applications or dedicated phone lines for convenient booking. When booking, indicate your pickup location and destination, and the taxi company will deploy a car to your area.

Taxi Fares:
Taxi prices in Malta are regulated and metered, providing fair and transparent pricing. Fares vary based on the distance traveled, time of day, and any extra services needed, such as baggage handling or help.

Ride-Sharing Apps: A Modern Alternative
Ride-sharing applications have grown more popular in Malta, giving a handy and cost-effective alternative to regular taxis. Popular ride-sharing applications like Bolt and Uber exist in Malta, enabling you to order a trip from your smartphone.

Using Ride-Sharing Apps:
Download the ride-sharing app of your choosing and establish an account. Once signed in, input your pickup location and destination, and the app will match you with a nearby driver. You may watch the

driver's progress in real-time and get reminders regarding their arrival.

Payment Options:

Payment for ride-sharing services is often done via the app, either by a connected credit or debit card or through a saved mobile wallet. The app will show the projected fee before you approve the trip, and money is immediately withdrawn upon conclusion of the route.

Additional Tips for a Smooth Taxi or Ride-Sharing Experience:

- **Have your destination ready:** Clearly convey your destination to the taxi driver or type it precisely in the ride-sharing app to prevent misunderstandings.

- **Consider local traffic conditions:** Taxis and ride-sharing cars may face delays during rush hour or in busy regions. Plan your route appropriately and provide additional time if required.

- **Respect local customs:** Be kind and respectful to taxi drivers and ride-sharing companies. Greet them politely, engage in conversation if appropriate, and thank them for their service at the conclusion of the voyage.

- **Enjoy the Maltese spirit of hospitality:** Embrace the kind and inviting character of Maltese people, particularly taxi drivers and ride-sharing companies. Engage in discussions, ask for advice, and absorb up the unique Maltese atmosphere.

Whether you prefer the ease of conventional cabs or the modernity of ride-sharing applications, Malta provides a number of alternatives to travel to its breathtaking landscapes and find hidden jewels. With their accessibility, convenience, and dependability, taxis and ride-sharing services give a seamless method to discover the island's rich legacy, lively culture, and spectacular natural beauty. Bon journey!

Malta Map View

As you travel Malta's map, let the island's rich tapestry lead your experience. Explore historic ruins, meander through sun-drenched plazas, and sample the flavors of traditional Maltese cuisine. Remember, Malta's map is not only a guide; it's an invitation to explore the island's fascinating essence and make experiences that will last a lifetime.

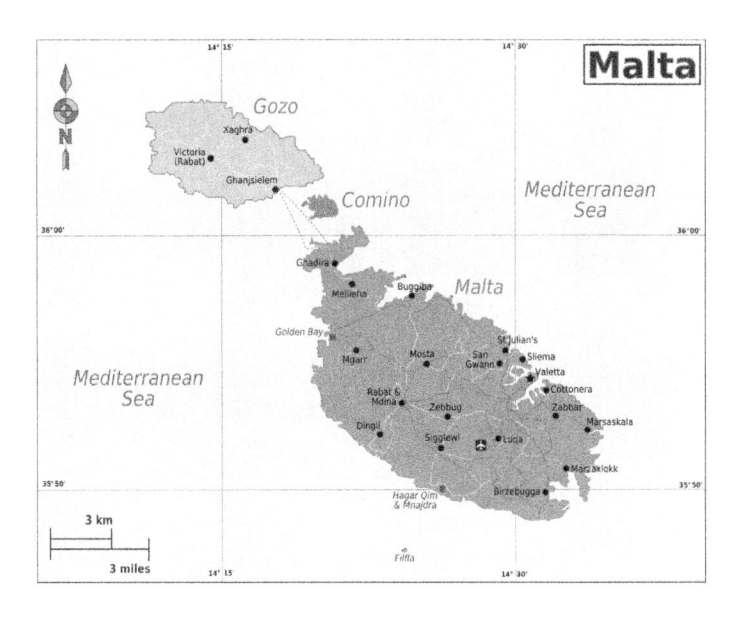

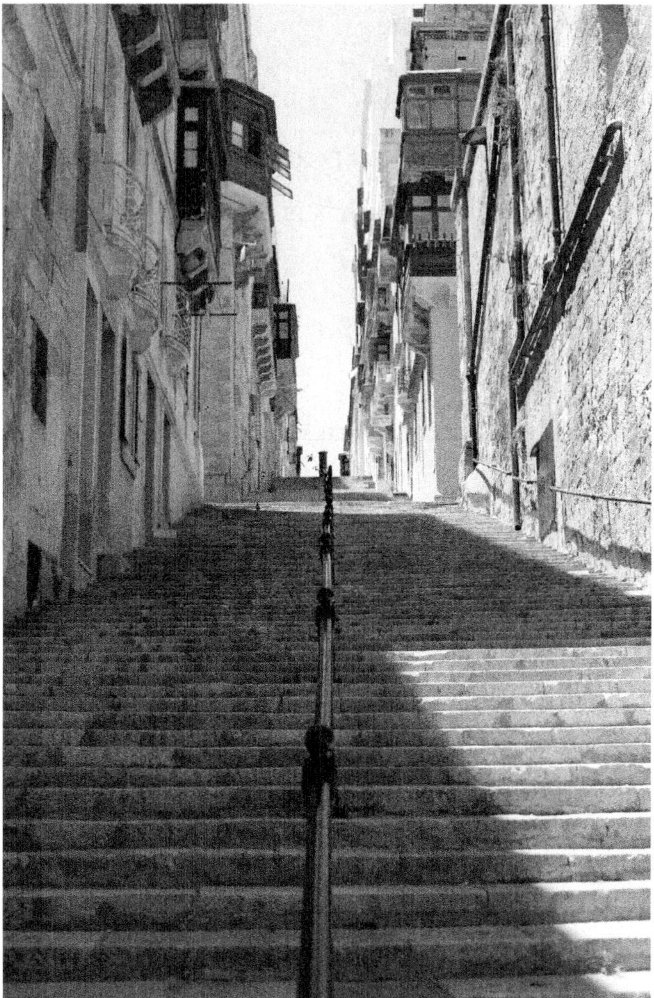

CHAPTER 4

Accommodation

Selecting the ideal lodging is vital, whether you want elegant hotels, quaint guesthouses, or warm flats, Malta provides a broad choice of alternatives to meet any traveler's preferences and budget.

Accommodation Options to Suit Every Style:
- **Hotels:** Malta provides an amazing assortment of hotels, catering to a broad range of interests and budgets. From opulent five-star resorts to quaint boutique hotels, you'll discover an accommodation that corresponds with your travel style and comfort needs.

- **Guesthouses:** For a genuine Maltese experience, guesthouses provide a warm and friendly environment. Often family-run, guesthouses give an insight into Maltese culture and local friendliness.

- **Apartments:** For individuals wanting additional freedom and flexibility, self-catering flats are a good solution. With fitted kitchens and comfy living areas, apartments provide a home-away-from-home experience.

- **Farmhouses:** Immerse yourself in the calm of the Maltese countryside by staying in a typical farmhouse. Surrounded by rolling hills and gorgeous scenery, farmhouses provide a unique and soothing refuge.

- **Hostels:** Hostels offer a budget-friendly choice for solitary visitors and groups. With shared rooms and public spaces, hostels provide a friendly and energetic environment.

Choosing Your Ideal Accommodation:

- **Consider your budget:** Accommodation charges vary based on the kind of accommodation, location, and time of year. Set a reasonable budget and study solutions that correspond with your budgetary limits.

- **Location:** Decide on the regions you intend to see and select lodging that is ideally positioned for your touring activities. Consider closeness to public transit, tourist sites, and amenities.

- **Amenities and Facilities:** Review the amenities and facilities supplied by each lodging choice to verify they match your requirements. Consider aspects such as Wi-Fi access, air conditioning, laundry facilities, and on-site eating.

- **Guest Reviews:** Read reviews from prior guests to acquire insights into the entire experience, service quality, and general satisfaction levels.

Additional Tips for a Hassle-Free Accommodation Experience:
- **Book in advance:** Especially during high season (June-August), reserving your hotel in advance assures availability and generally obtains lower prices.

- **Consider local regulations:** Some lodgings may have specified check-in and check-out timings, noise limits, or other limitations. Familiarize yourself with these tips to prevent hassles.

- **Respect local norms and etiquette:** Be careful of local traditions and politeness throughout your visit. Greet your hosts and other visitors pleasantly, be respectful of shared places, and enjoy the Maltese hospitality.

Embrace the warmth and generosity of Malta as you explore its stunning landscapes and find hidden jewels. With its broad choice of hotel alternatives, Malta provides an ideal home away from home, assuring a pleasant trip. Bon journey!

Luxury Hotels and Resorts

To complement your Maltese journey, the island provides an assortment of exquisite hotels and resorts, appealing to every traveler's need for rest, rejuvenation, and pleasure.

A Haven of Luxury and Comfort
From five-star coastal resorts to boutique businesses, Malta's hotels and resorts epitomize elegance, refinement, and individual service. Immerse yourself in a realm of calm, where every detail is thoughtfully constructed to assure your ultimate comfort and enjoyment. Step into a world of refined elegance, where contemporary design harmoniously mixes with Maltese charm, creating an environment of subtle grandeur and timeless refinement.

Unwind in Spacious Accommodations
Step into a world of large lodgings, where contemporary style harmoniously mixes with

Maltese charm. Each room is a haven of relaxation, furnished with opulent amenities, soft bedding, and spectacular views of the Mediterranean Sea or the island's scenic surroundings.

Pamper Yourself with World-Class Amenities
Indulge in a world of luxury in the hands of experienced therapists at the resorts' world-class spas. Unwind with restorative massages, energizing facials, and a range of wellness treatments meant to restore your body and mind to a state of perfect joy.

Culinary Delights to Tantalize Your Taste Buds
Embark on a culinary tour through Malta's rich gastronomic history. Resorts' fine-dining restaurants provide a tempting selection of local and foreign cuisines, made with fresh, seasonal ingredients and presented with creative flair. relish exceptional food, relish the atmosphere, and create wonderful dining experiences.

Recreational Activities for Every Taste

Whether you want adrenaline-pumping activities or quiet moments of relaxation, Malta's hotels and resorts cater to every choice. Dive into the crystal-clear waters of the Mediterranean Sea, indulge in a game of golf, bathe in the sun-drenched pools, or discover the island's hidden gems on guided tours.

Additional Tips for an Exquisite Hotel and Resort Experience

- **Book in advance:** Especially during high season (June-August), reserving your hotel in advance assures availability and generally provides lower prices.

- **Consider your budget:** Malta's hotels and resorts provide a broad variety of pricing ranges to suit every budget. Research solutions that fit with your budget limits without sacrificing quality and comfort.

- **Check for special bundles and promotions:** Many hotels and resorts offer seasonal packages and specials, giving extra value and potential for savings.

- **Communicate your preferences:** Inform the hotel or resort personnel about any particular requests or preferences, such as food restrictions or accessibility concerns, to guarantee a customized and accommodating experience.

As you immerse yourself in the world of Malta's finest hotels, appreciate the warmth and friendliness that is associated with Maltese culture. Enjoy the exceptional service, appreciate the amazing culinary delights, and allow yourself to be pampered and revitalized in the lap of luxury. Malta's luxury hotels are more than simply somewhere to stay; they are entrances to a world of exquisite elegance, customized service, and unique experiences. Bon journey!

Mid-Range Options

While the island provides a multitude of upscale hotels, it also has a broad selection of mid-range alternatives, catering to guests seeking pleasant stays without breaking the budget.

A Haven of Comfort and Value

Malta's mid-range lodgings provide a great combination of comfort, convenience, and value. From beautiful boutique hotels to family-run guesthouses, these places offer a warm ambiance and a customized experience, enabling you to thoroughly immerse yourself in the island's beauty and attractions.

Step into Spacious and Comfortable Rooms

Mid-range lodgings in Malta focus on your comfort, providing large and well-appointed rooms. Enjoy peaceful evenings on sumptuous mattresses, recline in pleasant living areas, and appreciate the thoughtful facilities supplied, providing a calm and delightful stay.

Explore Culinary Delights

Start your day with a delicious breakfast, generally included in the accommodation cost, to fuel your Maltese activities. Many mid-range lodgings provide in-house restaurants or collaborate with nearby eateries, giving a choice of eating alternatives to suit your taste and budget.

Discover Malta's Hidden Gems

Embrace the convenience of mid-range lodgings, frequently situated in central neighborhoods or within walking distance of major attractions. Explore the island's rich history, immerse yourself in its lively culture, and find hidden jewels with ease.

As you discover Malta's mid-range hotel alternatives, experience the warmth and kindness that is associated with Maltese culture.

Enjoy the courteous service, experience the local culinary delicacies, and allow yourself to be absorbed in the island's beauty and distinct character. Mid-range lodgings in Malta are more than simply somewhere to stay; they are doorways to a genuine Maltese experience, loaded with comfort, value, and great memories. Bon journey!

Budget-Friendly Stays

While the island provides a multitude of opulent hotels, it also has a broad selection of budget-friendly alternatives, appealing to those wishing to see Malta's treasures without breaking the bank.

A Haven of Affordable Comfort

Malta's budget-friendly lodgings focus on comfort and value, giving a warm environment and a customized experience. From small guesthouses to family-run hostels, these places give a comfortable base for exploring the island's breathtaking scenery and hidden jewels.

Step into Welcoming and Comfortable Spaces

Budget-friendly lodgings in Malta provide a warm and welcoming setting, assuring a comfortable stay. While facilities may vary, you'll find clean, comfortable rooms, generally with communal bathrooms, giving a quiet respite after a day of touring.

Explore Culinary Delights on a Budget

Many budget-friendly motels provide self-catering facilities, enabling you to make your own meals and save on eating prices. Alternatively, visit local restaurants and mercados (markets) to experience real Maltese food at moderate pricing.

Discover Malta's Enchanting Landscapes

Embrace the convenience of budget-friendly motels, frequently situated in central regions or within walking distance of key attractions. Utilize public transit, hire a bicycle, or explore on foot to discover the island's rich history, immerse yourself in its lively culture, and unearth hidden jewels.

As you tour Malta's budget-friendly lodgings, appreciate the warmth and kindness that is associated with Maltese culture. Enjoy the courteous service, experience the local cuisine, and allow yourself to be absorbed in the island's charm and distinct character.

Budget-friendly hotels in Malta are more than simply places to lay your head; they are entrances to a genuine Maltese experience, replete with affordability, value, and amazing memories. Bon journey!

Bed and Breakfasts

While Malta provides a wealth of lodging alternatives, bed and breakfasts (B&Bs) stand out for their intimate setting, personalized service, and ability to engage with local life.

A Home Away from Home

Step into the inviting embrace of Malta's bed & breakfasts, where every detail is painstakingly crafted to give a homelike experience. Enjoy the warmth and hospitality of Maltese families or individual hosts who take delight in sharing their expertise and affection for their island home.

Immerse Yourself in Cozy Accommodations

B&Bs in Malta provide a choice of accommodations to suit your interests, from lovely single rooms to warm family suites. Each accommodation is created with comfort in mind, giving a pleasant respite after a day of discovering the island's attractions.

Savor a Taste of Local Flavors

Wake up to a wonderful breakfast, generally made by your host, displaying the tastes of Maltese cuisine. Indulge in freshly made bread, traditional pastries, and local cheeses, setting the mood for a day of wonderful activities.

Embark on Authentic Experiences

Bed & breakfasts give a unique chance to engage with local life and obtain insider insights for discovering the island's hidden beauties. Your hosts will happily share their knowledge of local customs, traditions, and the finest locations to experience true Maltese culture.

As you experience the warmth and charm of Malta's bed and breakfasts, you'll discover the essence of Maltese hospitality. Enjoy the individualized attention, experience the local cuisine, and allow yourself to be welcomed into the heart of Maltese life.

Bed & breakfasts in Malta are more than simply places to stay; they are doorways to real experiences, packed with warmth, comfort, and amazing memories. Bon journey!

Self-Catering Apartments

While Malta provides a broad choice of lodging alternatives, self-catering flats stand out for their flexibility, freedom, and ability to completely immerse oneself in the local culture.

A Home Away from Home with Culinary Independence
Self-catering flats in Malta give a pleasant and accessible base for exploring the island at your own speed. With fully equipped kitchens, you have the opportunity to create your own meals, saving on eating expenditures and relishing the pleasures of local vegetables and markets.

Spacious and Well-Appointed Spaces
Self-catering flats provide a choice of layouts to meet your requirements, from modest studios to big family units. Each apartment is well-appointed with contemporary conveniences, guaranteeing a pleasant and peaceful stay.

Unveiling the Island's Treasures at Your Own Pace

Self-catering flats provide the opportunity to design your own schedule and discover Malta's breathtaking landscapes and hidden jewels at your own speed. From sun-kissed beaches to ancient ruins, the island's riches await your exploration.

Indulge in a Taste of Local Flavors

Visit local markets, filled with fresh food, and experience the flavors of Malta's gastronomic history. Experiment with local foods in your fully equipped kitchen, creating your own distinctive Maltese dining experience.

Additional Tips for Enjoying Self-Catering Apartments

- **Plan your food shopping:** Familiarize yourself with local markets and supermarkets to plan your grocery shopping properly.

- **Explore nearby eating options:** While self-catering affords freedom, don't miss out on enjoying the island's gastronomic wonders at local eateries.

- **Embrace the local spirit:** Engage with your neighbors, merchants, and other visitors, exchanging experiences and immersing yourself in the Maltese way of life.

As you enjoy the flexibility and convenience of self-catering flats in Malta, you'll discover the essence of Maltese hospitality. Embrace the native charm, appreciate the distinctive cuisine, and allow yourself to be fascinated by the island's unique character. Self-catering flats in Malta are more than simply somewhere to stay; they are entrances to a fully autonomous and immersive Maltese experience. Bon journey!

CHAPTER 5

Must-Visit Places

To guide your Maltese trip, here's a list of must-visit spots that will engage your senses and produce lasting memories.

Valletta: A UNESCO World Heritage Gem
Step into the heart of Malta's capital city, Valletta, a UNESCO World Heritage site that emanates beauty and elegance. Explore the city's defensive walls, dating back to the 16th century, and enjoy the spectacular architecture, a combination of Baroque, Mannerist, and Neoclassical styles. Visit the St. John's Co-Cathedral, a masterpiece of Baroque art, and marvel at the sumptuous interior filled with murals and delicate sculptures. Immerse yourself in the city's dynamic atmosphere, wandering along the busy streets packed with shops and cafés, and bask in the panoramic views of the Grand Harbor from the Upper Barrakka Gardens.

Mdina: A Tranquil Retreat in the Silent City

Venture inside the calm city of Mdina, popularly known as the "Silent City," set on a hill overlooking the Maltese countryside. Wander through the city's tiny, twisting lanes, surrounded by classic Maltese residences and ancient sites. Visit the Mdina Cathedral, a Norman masterpiece, and appreciate the panoramic views from the Mdina bastions. As you wander, let the peacefulness of the city embrace you, far apart from the hurry and bustle of contemporary life.

The Blue Lagoon: A Paradise of Crystalline Waters

Escape to the Comino Islands, a calm refuge in the Mediterranean Sea, and explore the magnificent Blue Lagoon. Embark on a boat ride to this hidden bay, where turquoise seas wash against immaculate coastlines and the sun paints the sky with colors of gold and blue. Take a refreshing bath in the crystal-clear seas, snorkel amid abundant marine life, or just sit on the smooth sand, taking in the quiet beauty of this natural paradise.

Megalithic Temples of Malta: Echoes of a Prehistoric Past
Embark on a voyage through time to the prehistoric past and discover the Megalithic Temples of Malta, six UNESCO World Heritage-listed buildings that stand as testaments to the architectural brilliance of Malta's ancient people. Discover the temples of Tarxien, Hagar Qim, Mnajdra, Ta' Hagrat, Skorba, and Ggantija, each with its own characteristics and intriguing allure. Wander among these megalithic buildings, marvel at the accuracy of their construction, and envision the life of the people who created them almost 5,000 years ago.

The Three Cities: Immerse Yourself in Maritime History
Venture across the Grand Harbor from Valletta and immerse yourself in the rich maritime heritage of the Three Cities: Senglea, Cospicua, and Birgu.

Explore the small alleyways adorned with classic Maltese cottages, fortified walls, and ancient sites. Visit the Inquisitor's Palace, a museum situated in the old headquarters of the Holy Inquisition, and dig into the city's unique history. As you travel around these wonderful cities, let the lively atmosphere and the tales inscribed in the stones take you back in time.

Exploring Malta's Natural Beauty:
Malta's stunning landscapes extend beyond its historical and cultural riches. Discover the island's natural beauty by trekking to these lovely places:

- **Dingli Cliffs:** Stand at the brink of the Dingli Cliffs, the highest point on the Maltese Islands, and see the stunning panoramic views of the Mediterranean Sea and the adjacent islands.

- **Ramla Bay:** Escape to the peaceful Ramla Bay, a sandy beach hidden inside a natural cove, surrounded by lush foliage. Relax on the silky sand, swim in the turquoise seas, and enjoy the quiet of this hidden treasure.

- **Imnajdra Walk:** Embark on a magnificent coastal stroll along the Imnajdra stroll, a footpath that twists along the cliffs, affording spectacular views of the sea and the historic Imnajdra Temple complex.

- **Malta National Park:** Immerse yourself in the natural splendor of Malta National Park, home to various flora and animals. Hike along the park's paths, explore the valleys and caverns, and discover the unique natural gems of Malta.

- **Blue Grotto:** Take a boat ride to the Blue Grotto, a natural grotto lighted by an underwater aperture, giving a fascinating effect of shimmering blue light.

As you discover these must-visit destinations in Malta, enjoy the warmth and friendliness of the Maltese people, sample the local food, and allow yourself to be charmed by the island's distinctive charm and rich legacy. Malta is a treasure trove of adventures waiting

Valletta - The Capital City

Malta's capital city, Valletta, is a UNESCO World Heritage site embellished with gorgeous architecture, medieval fortifications, and a dynamic cultural? life. Nestled on a peninsula overlooking the Grand Harbor, Valletta emits an irresistible beauty that has charmed travelers for generations. Embark on a tour through the city's intriguing streets and find the riches that await you.

Step into a Fortified Wonderland

Valletta's beginnings trace back to the 16th century when the Knights of St. John, a prominent religious and military order, converted the peninsula into a fortified bastion. As you tour the city, you'll be welcomed by an astonishing variety of fortifications, including the city walls, bastions, and gates. Admire the elaborate bastions that stand as quiet defenders of the city, and envision the wars that previously transpired behind their walls.

A Fusion of Architectural Styles

Valletta's architecture is a beautiful combination of Baroque, Mannerist, and Neoclassical styles, reflecting the city's rich history and cultural influences. Stroll down the city's main street, Republic Street, surrounded by gorgeous buildings and vibrant stores. Admire the grandeur of St. John's Co-Cathedral, a masterpiece of Baroque style, and marvel at its magnificent interior filled with murals and delicate sculptures.

A Hub of Cultural Delights

Valletta is a lively cultural city, providing a wealth of museums, theaters, and art galleries to visit. Delve into the city's rich history at the Malta National Museum, or immerse yourself in the realm of modern art at the MUZA. Visit the Manoel Theatre, a spectacular 18th-century theater, and enjoy a performance of opera, ballet, or drama.

Panoramic Vistas and Tranquil Gardens

Venture to the Upper Barrakka Gardens, a refuge of serenity in the hectic metropolis. As you meander through the gardens, filled with flowers and fountains, breathe in the panoramic views of the Grand Harbor, a stunning vista of the city and its surrounds.

Savor the Flavors of Malta

Valletta's culinary scene is a fascinating combination of traditional Maltese cuisine and cosmopolitan influences. Indulge in a substantial pastizzi, a delicious pastry filled with ricotta cheese or peas, or relish a classic Maltese fish soup, a tasty broth laced with local shellfish and spices.

Experience Maltese Hospitality

The warmth and openness of the Maltese people are reflected in Valletta's inviting environment. As you travel around the city's streets, engage in discussions with residents, listen to their experiences, and experience the authentic essence of Maltese culture.

Additional Tips for Exploring Valletta:

- Wear comfortable shoes since Valletta is a city best experienced on foot.

- Carry a reusable water bottle to remain hydrated, particularly during the hotter summer months.

- Take advantage of the hop-on, hop-off bus excursions to obtain an overview of the city and its key attractions.

- Immerse yourself in the local culture by attending a typical Maltese festa, a boisterous festival complete with music, food, and fireworks.

- Embrace the Maltese sense of relaxation and enjoy the tranquil pace of life in Valletta. Take your time to meander around the streets, discover the secret nooks, and absorb the distinctive beauty of this intriguing city.

Mdina - The Silent City

Perched on a hill overlooking the lovely Maltese countryside, Mdina, often known as the "Silent City," draws guests with its tranquil ambiance, enthralling history, and architectural magnificence. Once Malta's capital city, Mdina has retained its timeless charm, offering a glimpse into the island's rich heritage and unique character. Embark on a stroll through Mdina's quiet streets and uncover the treasures that await you.

Step into a Realm of Tranquility

As you reach the gates of Mdina, a sensation of peace floods over you. The city's name, meaning "city" in Arabic, accurately portrays its calm atmosphere. The small, twisting alleyways are free of the rush and bustle of contemporary life, replaced with a calm peace that begs you to sit down and absorb the moment.

A Journey across Time

Mdina's history extends back to the Phoenician period, and its rich legacy is visible in every area of the city. Stroll over the historic city walls, dating back to the 8th century BC, and envision the conflicts and sieges that once transpired inside these defenses. Visit St. Paul's Cathedral, a Baroque masterpiece created in the 17th century, and marvel at its beautiful carvings and gilded interior.

A Haven of Architectural Gems

Mdina's architecture is a beautiful combination of Norman, Baroque, and Neoclassical styles, reflecting the city's eclectic past. Explore the towering Vilhena Palace, a former seat of the Grand Masters of the Knights of St. John, and marvel at its majesty. Wander through the tiny alleyways lined with classic Maltese buildings, embellished with wooden balconies and colorful doors, each giving a touch of elegance to the city's surroundings.

Panoramic Views and Hidden Gems

Ascend to the Mdina Bastions, the city's defensive defenses, and be enchanted by the spectacular panoramic views of the Maltese landscape. On a clear day, you can even glimpse the neighboring islands of Gozo and Comino. Venture beyond the main highway and uncover hidden jewels nestled away in the city's labyrinthine alleyways, such as beautiful cafés, artisan stores, and tranquil courtyards.

Embrace the Silent City's Charm

Mdina's stillness is not a lack of sound, but rather a wonderful combination of peace and whispered storytelling. As you tour the city, listen to the echoes of the past, the soft rustling of leaves, and the distant sounds of church bells. Allow yourself to be engulfed by the city's tranquil environment and appreciate the unique appeal of the Silent City.

Additional Tips for Exploring Mdina:
- Wear comfortable shoes since Mdina's streets are paved with cobblestones.

- Take your time to walk around the city's small alleyways and find hidden jewels.

- Visit Mdina during the early morning or late afternoon to enjoy the city's calm environment at its fullest.

- Enjoy a classic Maltese supper at one of the city's lovely restaurants, enjoy the local delicacies, and engage in talks with the friendly people.

- Embrace the Silent City's unhurried pace of life and allow yourself to be transported to a period of calm and timeless charm.

Gozo Island

Nestled in the blue seas of the Mediterranean Sea, Gozo, Malta's second-largest island, is a captivating refuge of natural beauty, ancient history, and quiet charm. Often overshadowed by its busy sister island, Malta, Gozo gives a look into a slower, calm pace of life, luring guests with its rustic surroundings, intriguing sights, and kind hospitality.

A Retreat within Nature's Embrace
Gozo's natural beauty is a symphony of landscapes, from craggy cliffs and secluded coves to rich valleys and lovely farmland. Explore the majestic Dingli Cliffs, the highest point in the Maltese Islands, and marvel at the panoramic views of the Mediterranean Sea and the adjacent islands. Wander through the Ramla Valley, a green oasis filled with olive orchards and carob trees, and breathe in the quiet environment.

Untouched Beaches and Secluded Coves

Gozo's coastline is a sanctuary for beach lovers, providing a variety of quiet coves and sandy shorelines. Bask in the sun on the golden beaches of Ramla Bay, take a refreshing plunge in the turquoise waters of Xlendi Bay, or explore the hidden jewel of Dwejra Bay, noted for its distinctive rock formation known as the Azure Window.

A Journey through History's Footprints

Gozo's past is inscribed in its ancient ruins, picturesque towns, and traditional architecture. Visit the Ggantija Temples, megalithic buildings dating back to 3600-2500 BC, and marvel at the technical genius of Malta's ancient people. Explore the formidable walls and bastions of the Cittadella, the island's medieval capital, and envision the wars that once transpired inside these defenses.

A Haven of Cultural Delights

Gozo's cultural tapestry is created from traditional crafts, folklore, and vivid festivities. Visit the Ta' Djanni Windmill, a restored 18th-century windmill that serves as a tribute to the island's agricultural tradition. Immerse yourself in the local heritage by attending the annual feast of Saint George, a spectacular event full of music, fireworks, and traditional celebrations.

Savor the Flavors of Gozo

Gozo's gastronomic scene is a joy for foodies, delivering a taste of real Maltese cuisine. Indulge in a substantial plate of fresh local cheeses, relish a classic Maltese fish soup, or experience the island's characteristic meal, ftira, a delicious flatbread stuffed with different toppings.

Embrace Gozo's Warm Hospitality

The kindness and generosity of the Gozitan people are obvious in the island's calm environment and welcoming mood. As you travel around the villages, engage in talks with residents, listen to their experiences, and enjoy the authentic charm of Gozitan culture.

Additional Tips for Exploring Gozo:
- Rent a vehicle to explore the island at your own speed and uncover hidden treasures off the usual route.

- Take a boat journey to the adjacent islands of Comino and Cominotto for a day of sunbathing, swimming, and exploring the Blue Lagoon's crystal-clear waters.

- Visit the local markets to enjoy the colorful atmosphere and buy fresh vegetables, homemade crafts, and local souvenirs.

- Embrace the island's leisurely pace of life and appreciate the relaxing environment. Slow down, absorb the moment, and immerse yourself in the distinctive charm of Gozo.

Popeye Village

Nestled within the stunning surroundings of Anchor Bay, Malta, is Popeye Village, a mesmerizing theme park that takes guests to the enchanted world of Popeye the Sailor Man. Once a film set for the 1980 musical production of "Popeye," this lively hamlet has been turned into an interactive playground for children and adults alike.

Step into the World of Popeye and Olive Oyl

Wander through the quaint lanes of Popeye Village, dotted with rustic wooden buildings and ornamented with unique nautical décor. Discover Popeye's simple apartment, replete with his famous spinach can, and envision the exciting events that transpired here during the making of the movie.

Meet Popeye and His Friends

Engage in fun-filled exchanges with Popeye and his colorful ensemble of characters, including the ever-loving Olive Oyl, the mischievous Bluto, and the wise Wimpy. Capture amazing images with these legendary icons and create lasting memories of your vacation.

Embark on Exciting Adventures

Venture into Popeye's Playground, an area filled with exhilarating amusements for youngsters of all ages. Climb the towering Popeye Tower, cross the meandering Popeye Maze, and splash about in the Popeye Village Splash Pad.

Savor Culinary Delights

Enjoy a great dinner at one of the village's restaurants, providing a selection of delectable alternatives to fulfill every appetite. Indulge in Popeye's favorite spinach meals, enjoy traditional Maltese cuisine, or treat yourself to a delicious ice cream cone.

Unwind with Live Entertainment

Relax and take in the colorful atmosphere as you enjoy live entertainment throughout the day.

Witness thrilling performances by Popeye and his pals, participate in interactive activities, and let the vibrant music carry you to the heart of Popeye's universe.

Tips for a Memorable Visit to Popeye Village

- Purchase your tickets in advance to avoid lengthy lineups and save time.

- Plan your visit within the park's operating hours to ensure you have adequate time to experience all the attractions.

- Wear comfortable shoes appropriate for walking over rough surfaces.

- Bring sunscreen and a hat to protect yourself from the sun.

- Capture images and films to commemorate your memorable journey in Popeye Village.

Embark on a pleasant trip through Popeye Village and immerse yourself in a world of amusing adventures, engaging characters, and timeless memories. Discover the wonder of Popeye's universe and make memories that will last a lifetime.

Comino - The Blue Lagoon

Nestled in the shimmering waves of the Mediterranean Sea, Comino, Malta's third-largest inhabited island, is a serene haven recognized for its magnificent natural beauty, notably the hypnotic Blue Lagoon. With its crystal-clear turquoise seas, beautiful white sand shoreline, and quiet coves, Comino provides a retreat from the rush and bustle of daily life, encouraging tourists to immerse themselves in a world of peace and natural grandeur.

A Sanctuary of Tranquility

Stepping upon the beaches of Comino is like entering a sanctuary of peace. The island's car-free environment guarantees a calm ambiance, enabling you to reconnect with nature and relax among the gentle cadence of life. Stroll along the sandy beaches, the soft sand cushioning your feet while the calm waves lull you into a state of peace.

The Enchanting Blue Lagoon: A Must-Visit Paradise

The Blue Lagoon, Comino's crowning beauty, is a natural masterpiece that has enthralled tourists for years. Its crystal-clear blue waters, sparkling under the Mediterranean sun, form a fascinating scene that calls you to plunge in. The lagoon's secluded cove offers a serene retreat for swimming, snorkeling, and just basking in the sun's warmth.

Underwater Adventures: Unveiling the Marine Realm

Beneath the surface of the Blue Lagoon is a vivid underwater environment alive with colorful marine life. Don your snorkeling gear and start on an underwater excursion, finding a rainbow of fish dashing across coral reefs and exploring the secret depths of this natural aquarium.

Exploring Comino's Hidden Gems

Venture beyond the Blue Lagoon and find Comino's other hidden treasures. Hike around the island's pathways, taking you to hidden coves, scenic vistas, and the island's only inhabited settlement, Santa Marija Bay. Immerse yourself in the peacefulness of the island, where the leisurely pace of life enables you to properly enjoy the beauty that surrounds you.

Savor the Flavors of Comino

Comino's culinary culture reflects the island's simplicity and closeness to nature. Enjoy fresh seafood meals, experience the flavors of traditional Maltese cuisine, or indulge in a picnic basket full of local delicacies, relishing the flavors while you appreciate the stunning vistas.

Embrace Comino's Tranquility

As you explore Comino, let the island's calm wash over you. Slow down, disengage from the daily bustle, and immerse yourself in the present moment. Allow the peaceful flow of life to lead you, and experience the distinctive appeal of this quiet oasis.

Additional Tips for Exploring Comino:

- Plan your visit during the off-season (October to May) to avoid the peak crowds and enjoy a more serene experience.

- Rent a boat to explore the island's shoreline and find secluded bays unreachable by land.

- Bring along snorkeling gear to discover the spectacular marine life of the Blue Lagoon.

- Pack a picnic lunch or have a meal at one of the island's few eateries, relishing the tastes of the gorgeous surroundings.

- Embrace Comino's tranquil pace of life and allow yourself to genuinely relax and reconnect with nature.

Historical Sites

From ancient temples to medieval defenses, Malta's historical buildings remain as testaments to the island's intriguing history, providing tourists with a trip through time. Embark on a journey of these extraordinary locales and uncover the tales they speak.

Megalithic Temples of Malta: Echoes of a Prehistoric Past

Step into the fascinating realm of Malta's Megalithic Temples, six UNESCO realm Heritage-listed structures that remain as silent guardians of a bygone past. Dating back to 3600-2500 BC, these awe-inspiring monuments were erected by a competent ancient culture, their exquisite construction and high walls hinting at their superior knowledge and beliefs. Wander through the temples of Tarxien, Hagar Qim, Mnajdra, Ta' Hagrat, Skorba, and Ggantija, each with its own characteristics and intriguing appeal. Imagine the life of the people who erected these temples, their rituals, and their connection to the universe.

The Knights of St. John: A Legacy of Fortifications and Valletta

Delve into the age of the Knights of St. John, a strong religious and military order that dominated Malta from 1530 until 1798. Explore the majestic walls of Valletta, Malta's capital city, erected by the Knights as a bulwark against Ottoman invasions. Stroll around the city walls, observe the bastions and gates, and picture the wars that previously transpired behind these walls. Visit the Grandmaster's Palace, the former home of the Knights' Grand Master, and marvel at its splendor.

Mdina: A Journey through Time in the Silent City

Venture into the heart of Mdina, Malta's historic capital city, renowned as the "Silent City" for its serene environment. Wander through the small, twisting lanes adorned with classic Maltese dwellings and historic sites. Visit St. Paul's Cathedral, a Baroque masterpiece created in the 17th century, and marvel at its beautiful carvings and gilded interior. As you wander, let the peacefulness of the city embrace you, far apart from the hurry and bustle of contemporary life.

Hypogeum of Hal Saflieni: A Subterranean Mystery

Descend into the depths of the Hypogeum of Hal Saflieni, a UNESCO World Heritage site and one of the most intriguing archaeological sites in Malta. This underground structure, dating back to roughly 3000 BC, operated as a necropolis for Malta's ancient inhabitants. Explore the intricately carved chambers, linked pathways, and amazing artwork that cover the walls, revealing insights into the beliefs and rites of the ancient Maltese.

The Three Cities: Unveiling Maritime History and Fortifications

Venture across the Grand Harbor from Valletta and immerse yourself in the rich maritime heritage of the Three Cities: Senglea, Cospicua, and Birgu. Explore the small alleyways adorned with classic Maltese cottages, fortified walls, and ancient sites. Visit the Inquisitor's Palace, a museum situated in the old headquarters of the Holy Inquisition, and dig into the city's unique history. As you travel around these wonderful cities, let the lively atmosphere and the tales inscribed in the stones take you back in time.

Additional Tips for Exploring Malta's Historical Sites:

- Purchase a Multisite ticket to save money on admission costs to various historical sites.

- Wear comfortable shoes since you'll be doing a lot of walking.

- Carry a reusable water bottle to remain hydrated, particularly during the hotter summer months.

- Take your time to visit each location and admire its distinct characteristics and history.

- Engage with the people and ask questions to obtain a greater knowledge of Malta's rich past.

St. John's Co-Cathedral

St. John's Co-Cathedral, situated in the heart of Valletta, Malta's capital city, stands as a beacon of Baroque beauty and a tribute to the island's rich past. This beautiful cathedral, completed by the Knights of St. John between 1573 and 1578, is a must-visit location for any tourist looking to immerse themselves in Malta's cultural history and marvel at artistic magnificence.

A Symphony of Baroque Grandeur

Step inside the awe-inspiring interior of St. John's Co-Cathedral and be ready to be mesmerized by the symphony of Baroque grandeur that unfolds before you. The cathedral's opulent interior, filled with elaborate carvings, gilded sculptures, and a beautiful frescoed ceiling, is a monument to the creative skill of Mattia Preti, the Italian Baroque artist who masterminded its construction.

A Masterpiece of Light and Shadow

As you visit the church, let your eyes drift upwards, following the delicate features of the frescoed roof. The "Beheading of St. John the Baptist" by Caravaggio, the famed Italian painter, takes center stage, with its dramatic lighting and skillful use of chiaroscuro producing a mesmerizing display of light and shadow.

A Haven of Marble and Gilded Glories

The cathedral's interior is ornamented with an abundance of marble, its polished surfaces reflecting the ambient light and increasing the impression of grandeur. Gilded sculptures and elaborate carvings cover every corner, contributing to the cathedral's richness and evoking a feeling of awe and devotion.

A Journey through the Knights' History

As you visit the cathedral, take time to examine the various artworks and monuments that represent the history of the Knights of St. John. Their coats of arms, war scenes, and symbols of their religion cover the walls and floors, affording a look into the lives and triumphs of this strong order.

A Sanctuary of Peace and Spiritual Reflection

Despite its magnificence, St. John's Co-Cathedral emanates a feeling of peace and welcomes times of spiritual introspection. The warm glow of candlelight, the calm ambiance, and the tranquil beauty of the artwork create a sanctuary where visitors may rest, ponder, and connect with their inner selves.

Additional Tips for Exploring St. John's Co-Cathedral:

- Purchase a multimedia guide to increase your knowledge of the cathedral's history and artwork.

- Attend a concert or organ recital to experience the cathedral's acoustics and immerse yourself in the majesty of Baroque music.

- Dress modestly since the cathedral is a place of devotion.

- Be considerate to other guests and maintain a peaceful and meditative environment.

- Take your time to absorb the beauty and importance of this extraordinary masterpiece of Baroque art.

Hagar Qim Temples

Nestled atop a hill overlooking the Mediterranean Sea, the Hagar Qim Temples remain as quiet sentinels of Malta's intriguing ancient past. These megalithic buildings, dating back to 3600-3200 BC, are a UNESCO World Heritage site and a tribute to the inventiveness and architectural ability of Malta's ancient people. Embark on a trip through time and uncover the mysterious appeal of these awe-inspiring ruins.

A Portal to Prehistoric Times

As you approach the Hagar Qim Temples, picture yourself transported back in time, to an age when Malta was inhabited by a sophisticated society that had an incredible understanding of architecture and engineering. The temples themselves, made from gigantic megalithic boulders, create an aura of mystery and intrigue.

Exploring the Temple Complex

The Hagar Qim Temple complex comprises of five major temples, each with its distinct characteristics and layout. Wander around the Central Temple, the biggest of the group, and marvel at its massive façade and beautiful sculptures. Visit the East

Temple, famed for its trilithon entryway and the ornate pillar altar inside.

A Glimpse into Ancient Rituals

As you tour the temples, let your imagination run wild and visualize the rites and ceremonies that previously took place inside these hallowed places. The temples' alignment with the solstices reveals an awareness of astronomy and celestial occurrences, pointing to the complex religious system of Malta's ancient people.

Unveiling the Mysteries of the Fat Lady Statues

Among the most remarkable objects unearthed at Hagar Qim are the mysterious Fat Lady sculptures. These stylized female figurines, carved from limestone, are thought to symbolize fertility gods or priestesses. Their existence adds another depth of mystery to the temples, hinting at the religious beliefs and rites of the ancient Maltese.

A Sanctuary in a Picturesque Landscape

The Hagar Qim Temples are not merely archaeological remains; they are also a refuge of serenity in a magnificent setting. Stroll around the surrounding park, absorb the magnificent views of the Mediterranean Sea, and let the tranquil environment carry you away from the hurry and bustle of contemporary life.

Additional Tips for Exploring Hagar Qim Temples:

- Combine your visit with a tour of the neighboring Mnajdra Temples to explore two of Malta's most stunning ancient ruins.

- Wear comfortable shoes as the temple complex entails considerable walking over difficult terrain.

- Protect yourself from the sun with a hat and sunscreen, particularly during the heated summer months.

- Carry a reusable water bottle to remain hydrated.

- Embrace the mystery and fascination that surround these ancient remains and let your imagination take you back in time.

Natural Wonders

From majestic cliffs and isolated coves to lush valleys and secret caverns, Malta's natural beauties give a look into the island's various and compelling environments. Embark on an expedition to these extraordinary locales and uncover the riches that await you.

Dingli Cliffs: A Realm of Panoramic Vistas

Stand at the brink of the Dingli Cliffs, Malta's highest point, and be amazed by the spectacular panoramic views of the Mediterranean Sea and the adjacent islands. The cliffs, towering majestically from the beach, create a feeling of awe and majesty, while the steady cadence of the waves below offers a peaceful soundtrack.

Ramla Bay: A Secluded Paradise of Golden Sands

Escape to the isolated Ramla Bay, a quiet retreat situated inside a natural cove. As you approach, you'll be welcomed with the sight of golden beaches lapped by turquoise waves, providing a stunning scene that begs you to rest and unwind. Take a relaxing plunge in the crystal-clear seas, wander along the sandy coastlines, or just bask in the warmth of the Mediterranean sun.

Imnajdra Walk: A Coastal Trail with Enchanting Vistas

Embark on a magnificent coastal stroll along the Imnajdra stroll, a footpath that twists along the cliffs, affording spectacular views of the sea and the historic Imnajdra Temple complex. As you wander along the route, take in the fresh sea air, the vivid colors of the Mediterranean environment, and the calm of this pristine natural retreat.

Exploring Tranquil Valleys and Verdant Farmlands

Mistra Valleys: Embark on a picturesque trek through the Mistra Valleys, a sanctuary of natural beauty and historical value. Admire the green farmlands, examine the remnants of old temples, and snap magnificent images of the surrounding landscape.

Buskett Gardens: Immerse yourself in the calm of Buskett Gardens, one of the few wooded areas in

Malta. Stroll through the shaded pathways lined with old trees, have a picnic among the greenery, or uncover the secret fountains and caverns inside the gardens.

Verdala Palace grounds: Wander around the tranquil grounds of Verdala Palace, a 16th-century house surrounded by luxuriant foliage. Enjoy a leisurely walk around the fountains, sculptures, and groomed lawns, or uncover the secret bird refuge inside the grounds.

Malta National Park: A Haven of Diverse Flora and Fauna
Immerse yourself in the natural splendor of Malta National Park, home to various flora and animals. Hike along the park's paths, taking you to verdant valleys, secret caverns, and stunning overlooks. Discover the unique natural gems of Malta, from the rare Maltese Falcon to the aromatic wildflowers that beautify the countryside.

Blue Grotto: A Shimmering Spectacle of Underwater Light

Take a boat ride to the Blue Grotto, a natural grotto lighted by an underwater aperture, giving a fascinating effect of shimmering blue light. As you enter the cave, let the ethereal light wash over you and appreciate the exquisite rock formations that surround you. The Blue Grotto serves as a tribute to the force of nature and the beauty that lies buried under the surface.

Additional Tips for Exploring Malta's Natural Wonders:

- Rent a vehicle to explore the island at your own speed and uncover hidden treasures off the usual route.

- Bring along good shoes and sunscreen, since many of Malta's natural treasures entail walking and outdoor activities.

- Pack a picnic lunch or have a meal at one of the island's numerous eateries, relishing the taste of the gorgeous surroundings.

- Respect the natural environment and leave no sign of your stay.

- Embrace the peace and beauty of Malta's natural beauties and allow yourself to be fascinated by the island's different landscapes.

Blue Grotto

Nestled in Malta's southern coastline, the Blue Grotto stands as a captivating natural marvel, its enchanting beauty drawing people from near and far. This remarkable sea cave, embellished with bright blue colors and drenched in the Mediterranean sun, delivers an extraordinary experience, leaving its stamp on the spirit of every explorer who journeys inside its depths.

A Journey into an Illuminated Realm

Embark on a boat journey, floating down the blue seas of the Mediterranean, towards the entrance of the Blue Grotto. As you approach, suspense rises, and the instant you enter the cave, your eyes are welcomed with a captivating display. The sunlight streaming through an underwater aperture generates an ethereal glow, lighting the cave's interior with a symphony of dazzling blues.

A Canvas of Natural Splendor

The Blue Grotto's splendor goes beyond its brilliant waters. Gaze at the exquisite rock formations that adorn the cave's walls, fashioned by the unrelenting forces of nature over millennia. The interaction of light and shadow on these carved surfaces generates a captivating ballet of patterns, contributing to the cave's alluring charm.

A Tranquil Haven among the Azure Realm

As you glide into the Blue Grotto, a sensation of peace floods over you. The smooth cadence of the waves lapping against the cave walls offers a peaceful soundtrack, while the warm light of the lit waters produces an aura of calm. Allow yourself to be absorbed by the cave's peacefulness, leaving behind the hurry and bustle of the outside world.

A Treasure Unveiled

The Blue Grotto serves as a tribute to the strength and craftsmanship of nature. Its vivid colors, fascinating rock formations, and quiet environment provide an experience that stays long after your visit. As you emerge from the cave, leaving with you the memories of its captivating beauty, you'll understand why the Blue Grotto has become a beloved jewel of Malta's natural heritage.

Additional Tips for Exploring the Blue Grotto:

- Plan your visit around the early hours, when the sunlight's interaction with the water generates the most brilliant blue colors inside the cave.

- Opt for a traditional Maltese boat, known as a Luzzu, to enjoy the real charm of visiting the Blue Grotto.

- Combine your visit with a boat trip to other local destinations, such as the adjacent islands of Comino and Gozo, to make a great day of discovery.

- Capture the beauty of the Blue Grotto with pictures and movies, but remember to be courteous of the natural environment and avoid disturbing the fragile rock formations.

- Embrace the quiet of the cave and allow yourself to be fascinated by the stunning splendor of this natural treasure.

Dingli Cliffs

Rising magnificently from Malta's western shore, the Dingli Cliffs serve as a tribute to the island's natural magnificence. With their steep drops reaching heights of 253 meters above the glittering waves of the Mediterranean Sea, these awe-inspiring cliffs provide spectacular vistas and a look into Malta's intriguing geological history.

A Journey to the Island's Highest Point

Embark on a trek to the Dingli Cliffs, Malta's highest point, where you'll be welcomed with a vision of natural beauty that will leave you breathless. The cliffs, spanning along the shoreline for nearly 2 kilometers, present a magnificent vision of the Mediterranean Sea, the adjacent islands of Gozo and Comino, and the charming Maltese landscape.

A Sanctuary of Serenity among the Rugged Beauty

As you meander along the cliffs' edge, take in the fresh sea air, the soothing beat of the waves slamming on the rocks below, and the peacefulness that envelops this pristine natural retreat. Let the peace of the surroundings wash over you, leaving behind the hurry and bustle of daily life.

A Haven for Wildlife and Nature Lovers

The Dingli Cliffs are not merely a scenic sight; they are also a sanctuary for animals and environment lovers. Keep a watch out for the magnificent Maltese Falcon, flying through the sky, and observe the various flora that covers the cliffs, providing a splash of brilliant color to the rocky terrain.

A Landmark Steeped in History

The Dingli Cliffs have long had importance in Maltese history and culture. The region was formerly home to historic communities, and the cliffs themselves have acted as markers for sailors and navigators for centuries. Today, the cliffs endure as a symbol of Malta's natural beauty and tenacity.

Additional Tips for Exploring the Dingli Cliffs:

- Visit during the early morning or late afternoon hours to get the most beautiful views of the cliffs and the surrounding environment.

- Wear comfortable shoes and consider bringing a hat and sunscreen, since the location might be exposed to the elements.

- Bring along binoculars to maximize your wildlife-watching experience and glimpse the rare Maltese Falcon.

- Combine your visit with a tour of other local sights, such as the lovely hamlet of Dingli or the ancient temples of Ta' Hagrat and Skorba.

- Embrace the calm of the cliffs and allow yourself to be fascinated by the beautiful vistas and the peacefulness of this natural treasure.

CHAPTER 6

Coastal Attractions

Malta, an archipelago of beautiful islands situated among the turquoise seas of the Mediterranean Sea, is a refuge for lovers of coastal beauty. From craggy cliffs and isolated coves to golden beaches and secret caverns, Malta's coastline provides a symphony of natural beauties that call tourists to explore, relax, and immerse themselves in the island's distinctive appeal.

Golden Bay: A Paradise of Sun-Kissed Shores
Escape to Golden Bay, a paradise of golden dunes and crystal-clear seas, where the sun's warmth welcomes you to bask in its embrace. Stroll along the sandy sands, enjoy a refreshing plunge in the turquoise seas, or just rest in the quiet environment of this gorgeous beach paradise.

Ghajn Tuffieha Bay: A Hidden Gem of Serenity

Venture off the usual route and explore Ghajn Tuffieha Bay, a quiet treasure buried away within Malta's craggy shoreline. Descend a flight of stairs to reach this beautiful beach, where golden sands and turquoise seas make a picture-perfect environment for relaxation and exploration.

The Blue Lagoon: A Treasure of Comino

Embark on a boat journey to Comino, Malta's third-largest inhabited island, and explore the stunning Blue Lagoon, a natural wonder famous for its spectacular beauty. As you approach, marvel at the crystal-clear blue waters that sparkle under the Mediterranean sun, enticing you to plunge in and explore their refreshing depths.

Dingli Cliffs: A Realm of Panoramic Vistas

Stand at the brink of the Dingli Cliffs, Malta's highest point, and be amazed by the panoramic panoramas of the Mediterranean Sea and the adjacent islands. The cliffs, towering majestically from the beach, create a feeling of awe and majesty, while the steady cadence of the waves below offers a peaceful soundtrack.

Ramla Bay: A Sanctuary of Golden Sands and Tranquility

Escape to the isolated Ramla Bay, a quiet retreat situated inside a natural cove. As you approach, you'll be welcomed with the sight of golden beaches lapped by turquoise waves, providing a stunning scene that begs you to rest and unwind.

Embrace the Coastal Charm of Malta

Whether you want the excitement of water sports, the calm of hidden coves, or the majesty of craggy cliffs, Malta's coastline has something to offer every tourist. Let the island's seaside charm enchant you, and create memorable experiences among the splendor of the Mediterranean Sea.

Marsaxlokk Fishing Village

Nestled along Malta's southern coastline, Marsaxlokk Fishing Village stands as a refuge of peace and true maritime beauty. Its bright port, decked with colorful traditional fishing boats known as luzzus, looks into the island's rich nautical past and provides a mesmerizing setting for a leisurely walk or a lovely supper.

A Symphony of Colors and Cultural Traditions

As you approach Marsaxlokk, the brilliant colors of the luzzus, painted in tones of red, yellow, and blue, will quickly attract your attention. These historic fishing boats, with their characteristic eye-shaped insignia, are not only vehicles for catching fish; they are emblems of Malta's nautical history and a source of pride for the local fishermen.

A Haven of Fresh Seafood and Local Delicacies

Indulge your taste buds with the best seafood delights at Marsaxlokk's eateries and fishmongers. Savor the delicacies of locally caught fish, such as lampuki, tuna, and swordfish, served with traditional Maltese recipes. Don't miss the chance to enjoy the local delicacy, kannoli, a crispy pastry filled with sweet ricotta cheese, a lovely treat to complete your gastronomic trip.

Exploring the Sunday Market: A Cultural Extravaganza
Every Sunday morning, Marsaxlokk changes into a busy marketplace, a dynamic combination of local vegetables, handcrafted crafts, and souvenirs. Wander around the booths, packed with fresh fruits and vegetables, handcrafted Maltese lace, and traditional attire, and immerse yourself in the bright ambiance of this local market.

A Stroll around the Harbor and a Glimpse into Local Life
Embrace the calm of Marsaxlokk by wandering around its waterfront, while the fisherman prepare their boats for the day's catch. Observe the local ladies repairing fishing nets, the children playing on

the docks, and the seniors gathering in discussion, creating a scene that captures the real beauty of Maltese rural life.

A Sanctuary of Tranquility among the Bustling Coastline

Escape the noise and bustle of Malta's more tourist-frequented locations and find respite in the tranquil atmosphere of Marsaxlokk. The village's calm pace of life, its friendly residents, and its scenic port provide a welcome contrast to the busy city life, enabling you to completely immerse yourself in the island's quiet charm.

Additional Tips for Exploring Marsaxlokk Fishing Village:

- Visit on a Sunday morning to witness the colorful Sunday market and immerse yourself in the local environment.

- Engage with the people and ask questions to obtain a greater knowledge of Marsaxlokk's fishing traditions and the importance of the luzzus.

- Sample the fresh seafood delights at one of the harborside eateries, relishing the tastes of Malta's marine history.

- Capture the beauty of the multicolored luzzus and the lovely port with images and movies, but remember to be courteous of the local fisherman and their job.

- Embrace the quiet of the hamlet and allow yourself to relax among the original charm of Marsaxlokk, a place where time seems to slow down and the beauty of Malta's marine history comes through.

Golden Bay

Nestled along Malta's northern coastline, Golden Bay welcomes guests with its attraction of golden beaches, crystal-clear seas, and a laid-back attitude that promotes relaxation and regeneration. Whether you want the excitement of water sports, the calm of sunbathing, or the delight of discovering the surrounding natural beauties, Golden Bay provides an amazing coastal experience.

A Haven of Golden Sands and Turquoise Waters

Step into the smooth, golden beaches of Golden Bay and feel the warmth of the Mediterranean sun surround you. The soft waves lapping against the coast provide a peaceful soundtrack, while the great length of the bay, reaching around 500 meters, allows adequate room to spread out and enjoy the calm of the surroundings.

A Playground for Water Sports Enthusiasts

Golden Bay is a sanctuary for water sports aficionados, providing a range of activities to suit all levels of expertise. Embark on an exciting jet ski ride, test your balance on a stand-up paddleboard, or fly through the skies on a thrilling parasailing excursion. The quiet, shallow waters and mild sea wind make Golden Bay a great site to learn new water sports or just enjoy the pleasure of being out on the water.

A Sanctuary for Sunbathers and Relaxation

Golden Bay is a haven for sunbathers, giving adequate area to soak up the warm Mediterranean sun. Rent a sunbed and umbrella for a touch of comfort, or just roll down your towel on the smooth sands and let the lovely sea air caress you while you rest and refresh.

Exploring the Surrounding Beauty: A Walk to Ghajn Tuffieha Bay

Embark on a lovely coastal stroll from Golden Bay to the adjoining Ghajn Tuffieha Bay, a hidden jewel famed for its quiet mood and attractive surroundings. As you travel down the road, see the cliffs that surround the shore and take in the magnificent panoramas of the Mediterranean Sea.

A Culinary Adventure: Indulge in Local Delicacies

After a day of sun, sand, and sea, stimulate your taste buds with a great lunch at one of Golden Bay's restaurants. Savor the tastes of freshly caught seafood dishes, experience traditional Maltese cuisine, or treat yourself to a refreshing ice cream or a typical Maltese pastizzi, a savory pastry filled with ricotta cheese or peas.

Additional Tips for Exploring Golden Bay:

- Visit during the summer months to enjoy the full beauty of the warm sun and crystal-clear seas.

- Rent a sunbed and umbrella for enhanced comfort and shade during the busiest hours of the day.

- Bring along snorkeling gear to discover the abundant marine life in the shallow waters around the bay.

- Consider staying overnight in the adjacent town of Mellieha, which provides a choice of hotel options and eating experiences.

- Embrace the laid-back ambiance of Golden Bay and allow yourself to relax among the serene beauty of Malta's northern coastline.

Xlendi Bay

Nestled along the southern coast of Gozo, Malta's second-largest island, Xlendi Bay stands as a mesmerizing combination of natural beauty, a dynamic environment, and adventurous opportunities. Its picturesque location, embellished with golden dunes, turquoise seas, and attractive eateries, provides a refuge for leisure and exploration.

A Haven of Tranquility among the Rugged Coastline

As you reach Xlendi Bay, you'll be welcomed with a stunning vision of golden beaches running down the shoreline, softly caressed by the turquoise seas of the Mediterranean Sea. The bay's quiet environment, surrounded by majestic cliffs and beautiful surroundings, provides a pleasant reprieve from the rush and bustle of daily life.

A Paradise for Sunseekers and Water Sports Enthusiasts

Sink your toes into the smooth, golden sands of Xlendi Bay and feel the warmth of the Mediterranean sun embrace you. The bay's quiet, shallow waters and mild sea breeze make it a perfect site for sunbathing, swimming, and snorkeling. For those wanting a bit of thrill, a number of water activities, such as kayaking, paddleboarding, and jet skiing, are available.

Exploring the Underwater World: A Snorkeler's Paradise

Xlendi Bay's underwater environment is a treasure trove of natural beauties, ready to be found by snorkelers and scuba divers. Explore the brilliant coral reefs bursting with colorful marine life, marvel at the lively antics of fish dashing through the crystal-clear waters, and experience the excitement of meeting underwater caverns and rock formations.

A Culinary Adventure: Savoring Local Flavors

After a day of sun, sand, and sea, stimulate your taste buds with a great lunch at one of Xlendi Bay's restaurants. Savor the tastes of freshly caught fish dishes, experience traditional Maltese cuisine, or indulge in refreshing ice cream or a typical Maltese pastizzi, a savory pastry filled with ricotta cheese or peas.

Venturing Beyond the Bay: A Hike to the Xlendi Tower

Embark on a picturesque stroll from Xlendi Bay to the neighboring Xlendi Tower, a 17th-century watchtower that originally acted as a defense against invading invaders. As you approach the hill, observe the magnificent sights of the harbor, the surrounding landscape, and the neighboring islands of Comino and Malta.

Additional Tips for Exploring Xlendi Bay:
- Visit during the summer months to enjoy the full beauty of the warm sun and crystal-clear seas.

- Consider staying overnight at one of the quaint hotels or guesthouses bordering the bay, enabling you to completely immerse yourself in the calm environment of Xlendi.

- Bring along snorkeling gear to discover the abundant marine life in the shallow waters around the bay.

- Rent a boat and travel farther out to explore the coastline and uncover secret coves.

- Embrace the laid-back environment of Xlendi Bay and allow yourself to relax among the calm beauty and adventurous possibilities of Gozo's southwestern coastline.

Marsalforn Bay

Nestled along the northern coast of Gozo, Malta's calm island getaway, Marsalforn Bay stands as a compelling combination of natural beauty, laid-back charm, and a dynamic coastal vibe. Its exquisite environment, embellished with golden dunes, turquoise seas, and a lovely promenade, provides a place for relaxation, exploration, and reveling in the simple delights of a coastal retreat.

A Sanctuary of Sun-Kissed Shores

Step into the smooth, golden beaches of Marsalforn Bay and feel the warmth of the Mediterranean sun surround you. Stretch out on a nice sun lounger or just stretch out your towel on the smooth sands and soak up the warmth, while the calm waves lapping against the coast offer a relaxing soundtrack to your seaside relaxation.

A Playground for Water Sports Enthusiasts

Marsalforn Bay provides a range of water activities to suit all levels of skill, from relaxing paddles to exciting exploits. Embark on a kayaking or stand-up paddleboarding trip, gliding over the calm, turquoise seas and admiring the coastline from a new viewpoint. For those wanting a bit of excitement, take your hand at jet skiing or waterskiing, experiencing the rush of speed as you cut through the waves.

Exploring the Underwater Realm: A Snorkeler's Delight

Just under the glittering surface of Marsalforn Bay is a secret world of aquatic delights, ready to be explored by snorkelers and scuba divers. Explore the brilliant coral reefs overflowing with colorful fish, marvel at the delicate motions of jellyfish, and find the lively antics of crabs and mollusks zipping across the underwater terrain.

A Culinary Adventure: Savoring Gozitan Delights

After a day of sun, sand, and sea, stimulate your taste buds with a great lunch at one of Marsalforn Bay's restaurants. Indulge in the delights of freshly caught fish dishes, enjoy traditional Gozitan cuisine, or treat yourself to a refreshing ice cream or a typical Maltese pastizzi, a savory pastry filled with ricotta cheese or peas.

Wandering down the Promenade: A Seaside Stroll

Stroll along the lovely promenade that flanks Marsalforn Bay, soaking in the bustling atmosphere and magnificent vistas. As you go, explore the multitude of shops, cafés, and restaurants that line the shoreline, providing a beautiful combination of local crafts, souvenir treasures, and gastronomic pleasures.

Venturing Beyond the Bay: A Hike to the Zebbug Lookout

Embark on a picturesque stroll from Marsalforn Sea to the adjacent Zebbug Lookout, a vantage point affording stunning vistas over the sea, the surrounding countryside, and the neighboring islands of Comino and Malta. As you approach the hill, appreciate the lush flora, the typical Maltese farmhouses, and the serene serenity of the Gozitan scenery.

Additional Tips for Exploring Marsalforn Bay:

- Visit during the summer months to enjoy the full beauty of the warm sun and crystal-clear seas.

- Consider staying overnight at one of the delightful hotels or apartments bordering the bay, enabling you to completely immerse yourself in the calm environment of Marsalforn.

- Bring along snorkeling gear to discover the abundant marine life in the shallow waters around the bay.

- Rent a boat or kayak and journey farther out to find secret coves and explore the shoreline from a fresh viewpoint.

- Embrace the laid-back environment of Marsalforn Bay and allow yourself to relax among the calm beauty and beach appeal of Gozo's northern shore.

Sliema Promenade

Stretching along the northeastern coast of Malta, the Sliema Promenade is a compelling combination of urban flair and beach peacefulness. This colorful waterfront promenade, dotted with cafés, restaurants, and stores, provides a lovely getaway from the hectic city center, giving a spot to wander, relax, and enjoy the magnificent panoramas of the Mediterranean Sea.

A Seaside Haven among the Cityscape

Step onto the Sliema Promenade and let the calm sea air caress you as you wander down the concrete promenade. Admire the colorful variety of buildings that line the coastline, their design representing a combination of traditional Maltese style and contemporary influences. As you stroll, take in the magnificent views of the Mediterranean Sea, reaching out into the horizon, and generating a feeling of peace and unlimited possibilities.

A Playground for Leisure and Entertainment

The Sliema Promenade is a hive of activity, catering to a multitude of interests and inclinations. For those seeking relaxation, choose a comfy seat along the promenade and soak up the warm Mediterranean sun, or have a leisurely coffee or refreshing drink at one of the numerous cafés and restaurants bordering the waterfront.

A Culinary Adventure: Savoring Local Delicacies

Indulge in the delicacies of Maltese cuisine at one of the promenade's numerous eateries. Sample traditional foods such as lampuki pie, rabbit stew, or fenek (rabbit), experiencing the rich tastes and gastronomic traditions of the island. For a lighter treat, try a famous Maltese pastizzi, a savory pastry filled with ricotta cheese or peas, or indulge in cold ice cream to chill down on a scorching day.

Exploring the Surrounding Attractions: A Journey through Time

Venture beyond the promenade and explore the rich historical and cultural treasures that are within close reach. Visit the Fort Tigné, a 17th-century stronghold that originally acted as a barrier against invading armies, or visit the Parish Church of Jesus of Nazareth, a superb example of Baroque architecture with outstanding interior artwork.

A Sanctuary for Relaxation and Scenic Beauty

Amidst the rush and bustle of modern life, the Sliema Promenade serves as a refuge for leisure and calm. The mild sea air, the soothing sounds of the waves lapping against the coast, and the panoramic panoramas of the Mediterranean Sea create an environment of peace, enabling you to relax and escape the cares of daily life.

Additional Tips for Exploring Sliema Promenade:
- Visit during the evening hours to watch the promenade converted into a busy center of activity, with lit buildings and the warm glow of cafés and restaurants creating a mesmerizing mood.

- Rent a bicycle and enjoy a leisurely ride down the promenade, taking in the sights and sounds of this unique seaside road.

- Combine your stay with a boat tour to explore the adjacent islands of Comino and Gozo, finding secret coves and enjoying the beauty of the Maltese archipelago.

- Embrace the bustling atmosphere of the promenade and mingle with the people, learning about their customs and obtaining a greater knowledge of Maltese culture.

- Allow yourself to be captured by the beauty and charm of the Sliema Promenade, a site where urban dynamism combines harmoniously with the peacefulness of the Mediterranean Sea.

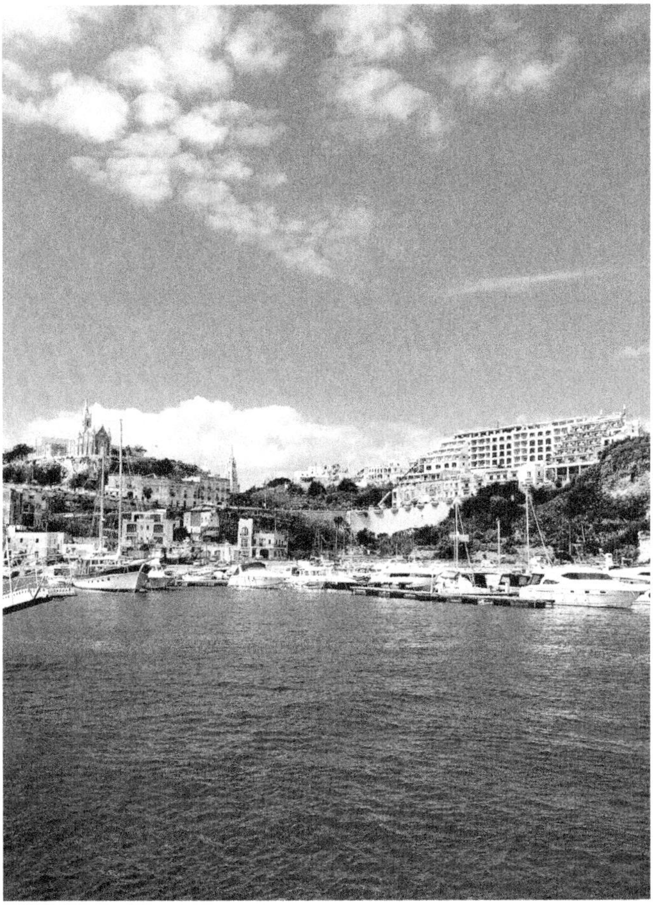

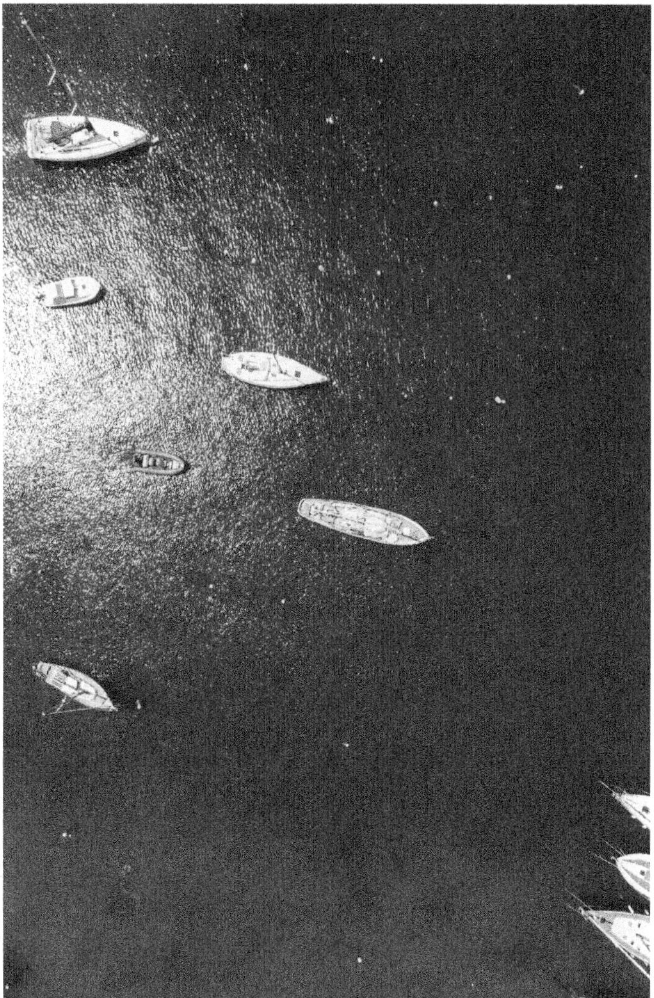

CHAPTER 7

Restaurants and Cuisine

Malta, provides a delicious gastronomic journey waiting to be explored. From traditional Maltese cuisine to worldwide cuisines, the island's restaurants cater to a range of tastes and preferences, offering a great dining experience for every guest.

Embracing Traditional Maltese Cuisine

Immerse yourself in the rich tastes of traditional Maltese cuisine, a symphony of influences from nearby Italy, Sicily, and North Africa. Sample the national cuisine, fenek (rabbit stew), loved for its soft flesh and rich smells. Indulge in lampuki pie, a flaky pastry packed with juicy fish, or try bigilla, a substantial dip prepared from dried wide beans and garlic.

Exploring International Delights

Venture beyond traditional Maltese dishes and experience the island's eclectic culinary culture. Savor the tastes of Italy with real pizzas, pasta dishes, and delectable risotto. Delight in the colorful scents of Indian cuisine, or delight in the fresh tastes of Mediterranean seafood delicacies.

Fresh Fish and Seafood: A Mediterranean Staple

Malta's seaside position offers an abundance of fresh seafood, making it a haven for fish lovers. Sample locally caught lampuki, tuna, and swordfish, served with traditional Maltese recipes. Enjoy the delicate aromas of octopus, frequently served grilled or in a stew, or experience the freshness of calamari, either fried or filled with delicious rice stuffing.

Local Delicacies and Sweet Treats

Don't miss the chance to enjoy local dishes that highlight the island's distinct culinary history.

Sample Maltese pastizzi, savory pastries filled with ricotta cheese or peas, or indulge in a refreshing imqaret, date-stuffed pastries coated in honey. For a sweet treat, try kannoli, crispy pastry tubes filled with creamy ricotta, or experience the delicate aromas of Maltese honey rings.

Dining with a View: Panoramic Settings

Enhance your eating experience by picking restaurants with magnificent views of the Mediterranean Sea. Imagine having a superb lunch while watching the shimmering waves, the craggy coastline, and the lovely towns that dot the landscape.

Maltese Cuisine

Embark on a delicious trip through Maltese cuisine, where traditional recipes and fresh, locally sourced ingredients come together to produce a symphony of sensations that will excite your taste buds and leave you hungry for more.

A Blend of Influences

Maltese cuisine is a compelling combination of influences from adjacent areas, reflecting the island's unique history and cultural links. Italian, Sicilian, and North African tastes mingle to produce a unique culinary character that is both recognizable and fascinating.

Embracing Rustic Simplicity

Traditional Maltese cuisine is defined by its rustic simplicity, employing fresh, locally obtained ingredients to produce substantial and tasty meals. Slow cooking techniques and the use of fragrant herbs and spices lend depth and richness to every mouthful.

Must-Try Delicacies

No gastronomic excursion to Malta is complete without experiencing some of the island's distinctive delicacies. Indulge in fenek (rabbit stew), the national cuisine, noted for its soft flesh and rich spices. Sample lampuki pie, a flaky pastry packed with juicy fish, or try bigilla, a substantial dip prepared from dried wide beans and garlic.

Sweet Indulgences

Satisfy your sweet taste with the island's exquisite pastries and sweets. Try Maltese pastizzi, savory pastries filled with ricotta cheese or peas, or indulge in a refreshing imqaret, date-stuffed pastries coated in honey. For a traditional delicacy, sample kannoli, crispy pastry tubes filled with creamy ricotta, or experience the delicate sweetness of Maltese honey rings.

Tips for a Delightful Culinary Adventure

- Engage with the pleasant staff or seek suggestions from locals and other visitors to find hidden gastronomic treasures and traditional Maltese gastronomy.

- Venture beyond the tourist districts to visit local eateries and enjoy the authentic flavors of Maltese food.

- Be experimental and try different meals, enabling yourself to be surprised and thrilled by the island's gastronomic variety.

- Embrace the Maltese custom of sharing meals with friends and family, providing a memorable and communal dining experience.

- Savor every taste, savoring the fresh ingredients, time-honored recipes, and love that goes into crafting each meal.

- Dress accordingly, as the restaurant maintains a sophisticated environment perfect for special events and festivities.

- Allow yourself to be fascinated by the spectacular views of the island, offering a genuinely memorable dining experience that marries culinary quality with natural beauty.

Popular Restaurants

Malta, an archipelago of beautiful islands situated among the turquoise seas of the Mediterranean Sea, is a destination for fans of gastronomic delicacies. From traditional Maltese food to foreign cuisines, Malta's restaurants cater to a range of tastes and preferences, offering a great dining experience for every tourist.

Embracing Tradition at Ta' Marija Restaurant
Step back in time and immerse yourself in the rich tastes of traditional Maltese cuisine at Ta' Marija Restaurant, a family-run restaurant set in the heart of St. Paul's Bay. For almost 60 years, Ta' Marija has been offering you traditional cuisine created with fresh, locally sourced ingredients. Sample their distinctive fenek (rabbit stew), appreciate the delicate aromas of lampuki pie, or indulge in a hefty bowl of bigilla, a typical Maltese dip.

A Culinary Journey at Tarxien Restaurant

Venture beyond the tourist sites and find Tarxien Restaurant, a hidden treasure nestled away in the tranquil village of Tarxien. This award-winning business prides itself on utilizing the freshest seasonal ingredients to produce unique and tasty Mediterranean cuisine. Their menu features a scrumptious assortment of seafood, pasta, and meat dishes, all made with love and a bit of contemporary flair.

A Culinary Haven at Caviar House & Vodka Bar

Step into a world of gastronomic refinement and pleasure at Caviar House & Vodka Bar, situated in the heart of St. Julians. This luxury venue provides a sophisticated dining experience, with a menu offering excellent caviar, beautiful seafood, and delectable steaks. Their enormous vodka range, comprising over 100 kinds, wonderfully complements their gourmet delights.

A Taste of Italy at Trattoria del Cuore

Indulge your taste buds with real Italian food at Trattoria del Cuore, a lovely restaurant hidden in the medieval town of Valletta. Their menu comprises traditional Italian meals created using fresh, locally sourced ingredients. Sample their wood-fired pizzas, relish their handmade pasta, or indulge in their delectable meat and seafood delicacies.

A Culinary Oasis at Rampila Restaurant

Escape the hustle and bustle of the city and discover serenity at Rampila Restaurant, set inside the medieval walls of the Cittadella in Victoria, Gozo. This unique restaurant provides a calm setting and a menu that highlights the finest of Maltese and Gozitan cuisine. Their meals are produced using fresh, local ingredients and reflect the island's unique culinary tradition.

Cafes

Malta, provides an abundance of quaint cafés to suit all tastes and inclinations. From indulging in rich, fragrant coffee and scrumptious pastries to relishing cool drinks and light snacks among a relaxing ambiance, Malta's thriving cafe scene delivers a fascinating and engaging experience for visitors wishing to immerse themselves in the island's culture and customs.

Embrace the Charm of Valletta's Historic Cafes

- **Caffe Cordina:** Step inside the historic Caffe Cordina, a Valletta institution since 1831, and discover the charm of traditional Maltese coffee culture. Admire the magnificent decor, sip a traditional cappuccino, and indulge in freshly prepared sweets.

- **The Trapeze Bar:** Venture to the bustling Trapeze Bar, a favorite destination for residents and visitors alike. Enjoy a refreshing beverage, eat a full meal, and absorb the vibrant environment.

- **Lot Sixty-One:** Immerse yourself in the sophisticated environment of Lot Sixty-One, recognized for its beautifully prepared coffee and exquisite pastries. Discover a chosen range of coffee beans, indulge in a wonderful flat white, and enjoy the dynamic environment.

- **Cafe Jubilee:** Venture to the bustling Cafe Jubilee, a favorite destination for residents and visitors alike. Enjoy a refreshing iced coffee, eat a big meal, and take in the vibrant environment.

Explore the Diverse Cafes in Sliema and St. Julian's

- **Cafe Ole:** Discover Cafe Ole, a hidden treasure in Sliema, famed for its welcoming environment and great coffee. Indulge in a delicious coffee, eat a small snack, and relax in the pleasant surroundings.

- **Fontanella Tea Garden:** Ascend the bastions of Mdina, Malta's old capital, and uncover the lovely Fontanella Tea Garden. Admire the panoramic vistas, sip a crisp lemonade, and indulge in a typical Maltese pastizzi.

- **Talbot and Bons:** Immerse yourself in the artistic environment of Talbot & Bons, a Sliema café recognized for its innovative ideas and exquisite sweets. Discover a blend of Maltese and foreign cuisines, have a refreshing iced tea, and indulge in handcrafted sweets and pastries.

- **Twenty-Two:** Discover Twenty Two, a contemporary rooftop bar in St. Julian's, noted for its breathtaking views of the Maltese coastline. Sip on a specialty drink, enjoy live music, and experience the spectacular sunsets.

Cafe Society: Immerse yourself in the classic sensations of Cafe Society, a vintage-inspired pub with a distinct ambiance. Discover a chosen range of beverages, eat a wonderful burger, and relax in the warm surroundings.

Venture Beyond the Tourist Hubs and Discover Local Favorites

- **Debbies Cafe:** Explore Debbies Cafe, a local favorite in St. Paul's Bay, noted for its friendly friendliness and tasty breakfast offerings. Savor a hefty omelet, taste a fluffy pancake, and start your day with a delicious coffee.

- **Kinnie Cafe Milk & Coffee:** Discover Kinnie Cafe Milk & Coffee, a quaint location in St. Paul's Bay, noted for its distinctive Maltese specialty drink, Kinnie. Indulge in a cool Kinnie milkshake, try a typical Maltese ftira, and experience the unique local flavor.

- **Cafe Maroc:** Venture to Cafe Maroc in Birgu, a lovely village steeped in history, and enjoy a combination of Moroccan and Maltese cuisine. Savor a classic Moroccan mint tea, savor a range of desserts, and immerse yourself in the unique ambiance.

Tips for Enjoying Malta's Cafe Scene

- Embrace the calm pace of Maltese cafés and relish the experience.

- Be respectful of local customs and traditions, such as greeting café personnel with a cheerful "bonjour" (good day) or "bonsoir" (good evening).

- Explore cafés outside the tourist centers and uncover hidden treasures favored by locals.

- Capture images and write your café encounters to build treasured memories.

- Indulge in traditional Maltese pastries and drinks to completely immerse yourself in the local culture.

Embark on a wonderful tour through Malta's cafés and find a refuge for coffee enthusiasts and casual cappuccino seekers alike. From ancient businesses to contemporary havens, Malta's diversified cafe scene gives a wonderful and engaging experience that represents the island's rich legacy and dynamic culture.

Ta' Kris

Nestled among the busy streets of Sliema, Malta, Ta' Kris Restaurant shines as a culinary beacon, enticing tourists to embark on a delicious trip into the heart of Maltese cuisine. With its friendly environment, time-honored recipes, and sincere devotion to fresh, locally sourced ingredients, Ta' Kris has earned its status as a valued local gem, delivering a genuine taste of Maltese culinary history.

A Culinary Legacy in the Making

Step inside Ta' Kris and be transported to a bygone period, when the walls ooze the warmth and charm of an ancient Maltese bakery. The restaurant's long history extends back to the 1950s, when it acted as a neighborhood center, supplying freshly baked bread and pastries to the local population. Today, Ta' Kris has developed into a gastronomic destination, keeping the spirit of its tradition while embracing the expanding preferences of contemporary diners.

A Culinary Symphony of Traditional Flavors

Ta' Kris' cuisine is a tribute to the island's rich culinary history, displaying a symphony of traditional Maltese dishes created using time-honored techniques and fresh, locally produced ingredients. Indulge in the luscious scents and tastes of fenek (rabbit stew), a national dish famous for its soft flesh and thick sauce. Savor the delicate tastes of lampuki pie, a flaky pastry packed with juicy fish, or indulge in the robust goodness of bigilla, a traditional Maltese dip prepared from dried wide beans and garlic.

A Culinary Canvas for Local Produce

Ta' Kris' devotion to fresh, locally obtained ingredients is obvious in every meal. The restaurant works closely with local farmers and fishermen to guarantee that its kitchen is constantly equipped with the best seasonal food and the freshest catch from the Mediterranean Sea. This attention to excellence means that every meal is filled with the bright tastes and smells of the Maltese terroir.

A Culinary Haven for All

Ta' Kris welcomes visitors with wide arms, catering to a diversity of interests and preferences. Whether you want the robust pleasure of traditional Maltese dining, the delicate tastes of fish delicacies, or the comfort of handmade pasta meals, Ta' Kris offers something to tickle every pallet.

Embracing the Maltese Culinary Tradition

At Ta' Kris, eating is more than simply a meal; it's an engaging experience that encompasses the spirit of Maltese culture and hospitality. The restaurant's warm and friendly environment, along with the dedicated service of its personnel, offers a pleasant setting where customers may fully experience the art of Maltese food.

The Harbour Club

Perched along the magnificent waterfront of Valletta, Malta's enchanting capital city, The Harbour Club stands as a culinary beacon, luring guests with its promise of sophisticated cuisine and stunning vistas. This esteemed restaurant, housed within a beautifully restored 18th-century waterfront building, offers a harmonious blend of culinary excellence, historical charm, and panoramic vistas of the Grand Harbour, creating an unforgettable dining experience that encapsulates the essence of Malta's rich heritage and vibrant culture.

A Culinary Sanctuary among Historical Charm
As you stroll inside The Harbour Club, you'll be immersed in an environment of sophisticated elegance and subtle grandeur. The restaurant's decor conveys a feeling of timeless elegance, with its exposed stone walls, arched doors, and warm, welcoming lighting. The meticulously designed décor, incorporating traditional Maltese accents and

contemporary design elements, produces a harmonic combination of old and new, reflecting the city's rich history and its dynamic current energy.

A Symphony of Culinary Delights

The Harbour Club's culinary offerings are a tribute to the chef's love for fresh, locally produced ingredients and inventive Mediterranean cuisine. The menu presents a delightful selection of meals, each expertly prepared to tickle the taste senses and create a symphony of tastes. Indulge in the delicate tastes of locally caught fish, appreciate the succulent scents of grilled meats, or indulge in the brilliant colors and textures of fresh Mediterranean salads.

A Culinary Journey with Panoramic Vistas

The Harbour Club's dining experience goes beyond its exceptional food, giving spectacular panoramic views of the Grand Harbour. As you taste your dinner, you'll be entranced by the stunning views of the busy port, the ancient fortifications that surround the shoreline, and the beautiful waves of the Mediterranean Sea. This unique location perfectly marries culinary quality with natural beauty, producing an extraordinary dining experience that is really one of a kind.

A Culinary Haven for Celebrations and Special Occasions

The Harbour Club is a great place for celebrating life's important events, whether it's a romantic anniversary, a milestone birthday, or a private gathering with friends and family. The restaurant's private dining room, with its intimate location and breathtaking views of the Grand Harbour, offers the ideal background for making treasured moments.

Noni

Nestled within the colorful streets of Valletta, Malta's beautiful capital city, Noni Restaurant stands as a culinary jewel, calling tourists to go on a delicious trip into the heart of Maltese food. With its friendly environment, unique culinary creations, and passionate devotion to fresh, locally sourced ingredients, Noni has earned its status as a cherished local favorite, delivering a genuine taste of Malta's gastronomic tradition with a touch of contemporary flair.

A Culinary Oasis in the Historic City Center

Step inside Noni and be taken to a small dining hideaway, where the walls convey a feeling of subtle elegance and modern appeal. The restaurant's décor, incorporating exposed stone walls, gentle lighting, and splashes of brilliant colors, offers a friendly setting that sets the scene for an exceptional gastronomic experience.

A Culinary Symphony of Tradition and Innovation

Noni's menu is a tribute to the chef's enthusiasm for recreating traditional Maltese cuisine with a touch of contemporary flair. The meals are expertly created using fresh, locally sourced ingredients, ensuring that each mouthful is filled with the bright tastes and aromas of the Maltese terroir. From delicate seafood delicacies to robust beef meals and a selection of vegetarian alternatives, Noni's culinary innovations appeal to a varied spectrum of tastes and preferences.

A Culinary Canvas for Local Artisanship

Noni's devotion to local products and artisanal workmanship is obvious in every part of the dining experience. The restaurant interacts closely with local farmers, fishermen, and craftsmen to obtain the freshest seasonal products and exhibit the originality and expertise of Maltese workmanship. This attention to excellence guarantees that every meal is a monument to the island's rich culinary tradition and its enthusiasm for fresh, genuine tastes.

A Culinary Haven for Discerning Palates

Noni welcomes visitors with open arms, catering to discriminating palates seeking an upgraded dining experience that highlights the essence of Maltese cuisine. Whether you seek the delicate tastes of seafood, the substantial comfort of traditional Maltese cooking, or the inventive concoctions that demonstrate the chef's culinary expertise, Noni offers something to tempt every pallet.

Embracing the Maltese Culinary Tradition

At Noni, eating is more than simply a meal; it's an entire experience that encompasses the spirit of Maltese culture and hospitality. The restaurant's warm ambiance, along with the enthusiastic service of its personnel, offers a welcoming setting where customers can fully experience the art of Maltese food, presented with a modern touch.

Street Food Delights

While its restaurants provide an assortment of sophisticated dining experiences, it's the island's street food sector that embodies the spirit of Maltese culture and cuisine. From savory pastries to fresh seafood specialties, Malta's street food is a symphony of flavor and tradition, delivering a pleasant tour through the island's culinary legacy.

Pastizzi: The Quintessential Maltese Snack

No journey of Maltese street cuisine is complete without indulging in pastizzi, the island's signature savory pastry. These little, golden-brown delicacies are stuffed with a variety of delicious fillings, including ricotta cheese, peas, or a mixture of both. Found in every part of Malta, pastizzi are a staple snack, delivering a pleasant nibble on the move.

Bigilla: A Flavorful Dip with a Rustic Charm

Bigilla, a substantial dip prepared from dried wide beans, garlic, and herbs, is a cherished Maltese staple. Its rich, savory taste and rustic texture make it a favorite companion to fresh bread or crackers. Often served as part of an antipasti plate, bigilla is a remarkable tribute to Maltese culinary tradition.

Hobz biz-Zejt: A Taste of Maltese Simplicity

Hobz biz-Zejt, a typical Maltese sandwich, is a monument to the island's fondness for basic, tasty ingredients. This rustic sandwich contains thick slices of Maltese bread, drizzled with olive oil and topped with a generous layer of juicy tomatoes, fresh capers, and a sprinkling of oregano. Its simple preparation and fresh ingredients give it a real taste of Malta's culinary essence.

Imqaret: A Sweet Indulgence with a Date-Filled Surprise

Imqaret, little, diamond-shaped pastries, provide a wonderful sweet treat on Malta's streets. These pastries are filled with a typical date paste, frequently flavored with orange zest and cinnamon, and then dipped in honey for an extra touch of sweetness. Imqaret are often consumed throughout the colder months, notably around Christmas and New Year's, making them a seasonal delicacy that reflects the warmth and comfort of Maltese customs.

Fenek (Rabbit Stew): A Hearty Culinary Tradition

Fenek, a traditional rabbit stew, is considered Malta's national dish. This hearty stew is cooked with rabbit meat, tomatoes, onions, garlic, and a combination of fragrant herbs, resulting in a rich, savory meal that has been loved by generations of Maltese families. Fenek is commonly eaten with macaroni or rice, making it a cozy and delicious dinner.

Street Food Markets: A Hub of Culinary Discovery

Malta's street food markets are a dynamic center of gastronomic discovery, providing an assortment of local specialties and a taste of the island's many culinary influences. These crowded markets, generally set up in town squares or near prominent tourist destinations, offer an immersive experience, enabling you to try a variety of street cuisine while soaking up the colorful ambiance.

Food and Wine Festivals

Malta, provides a plethora of food and wine festivals to satisfy all tastes and inclinations. From celebrating local delicacies and traditional cooking techniques to sampling international flavors and indulging in world-class wines, Malta's vibrant culinary scene provides a delightful and enriching experience for those seeking to immerse themselves in the island's rich heritage and diverse gastronomy.

Embark on a Culinary Journey at Malta's Premier Festivals

- **Malta International Food Festival:** Immerse yourself in the biggest and most popular cuisine festival in Malta, held annually in Valletta. Discover a broad choice of cuisines from across the globe, sample local specialties, and enjoy live entertainment in a festive environment.

- **Delicata Classic Wine Festival:** Explore the world of Maltese wine at the Delicata

Classic Wine Festival, held yearly in Valletta's Upper Barrakka Gardens. Sample award-winning wines from local vineyards, engage in delectable food pairings and experience stunning views of the Grand Harbour.

- **Farsons Beer Festival:** Unleash your inner beer connoisseur at the Farsons Beer Festival, held yearly at Ta' Qali National Park. Discover a large range of local and foreign beers, eat traditional Maltese food, and enjoy live music and entertainment.

Venture Beyond the Main Events and Discover Hidden Gems

- **Marsovin Wine Festival:** Immerse yourself in the rich winemaking traditions of Marsaxlokk, a typical fishing community, during the annual Marsaforn Wine Festival. Sample a selection of Maltese wines, eat local seafood specialties and experience the unique ambiance of this charming town.

- **Earth Garden Festival:** Embrace sustainability and conscientious living at the Earth Garden Festival, held yearly at Ta' Qali National Park. Discover organic food vendors, attend lessons on eco-friendly techniques, and enjoy live music and entertainment.

- **Strawberry Festival:** Indulge in the delicious joys of the Strawberry Festival, held annually in Mġarr, a lovely town famed for its strawberry farming. Sample strawberry-themed delicacies, enjoy live entertainment, and engage in exciting activities for the entire family.

Experience the Culinary Delights of Gozo
- **Malta International Food Festival Gozo Edition:** Discover the distinct culinary

traditions of Gozo at the Malta International Food Festival Gozo Edition, held yearly in Xewkija. Savor traditional Gozitan cuisine, experience worldwide flavors, and enjoy live entertainment within a joyful environment.

- **Festa Majjstral:** Immerse yourself in the vivid Festa Majjstral, held yearly in Mġarr, Gozo, a celebration of Gozo's patron saint, St. Peter and St. Paul. Discover traditional food vendors, sample local specialties, and join in vibrant processions and fireworks displays.

Tips for Enjoying Malta's Food and Wine Festivals
- Plan your festival itinerary in advance to guarantee you don't miss out on your favorite events.

- Purchase tokens or tickets in advance to avoid lengthy lineups and save time.

- Pace yourself and taste a range of items to properly enjoy the unique gastronomic landscape.

- Engage with local vendors and learn about the history and customs behind the dishes.

- Create treasured memories by collecting images and writing your festival experiences.

Embark on a delicious gastronomic tour through Malta's food and wine festivals and explore a world of tastes, customs, and vivid festivities. From worldwide cuisines to local specialties, Malta's diversified culinary scene gives an amazing experience that represents the island's rich history and passionate love for food and wine.

CHAPTER 8

Itinerary Suggestions

Day 1: Exploring the Charming Capital of Valletta

- **Morning:** Immerse yourself in the ancient heart of Malta by touring the UNESCO-listed walled city of Valletta. Wander around the small alleyways lined with attractive houses, see the breathtaking Grand Harbor vistas, and visit the St. John's Co-Cathedral, a marvel of Baroque architecture.

- **Afternoon:** Take a leisurely walk down the Sliema Promenade, admiring the magnificent views of the Mediterranean Sea and the bustling ambiance of this coastal town. Indulge in a wonderful meal at one of the numerous cafés or eateries along the waterfront.

- **Evening:** Experience the exciting nightlife of Malta by traveling to St. Julian's, a popular center for bars, clubs, and restaurants. Enjoy a dynamic supper with a view of Spinola Bay and immerse yourself in the bustling atmosphere of this seaside town.

Day 2: Unveiling the Hidden Gems of Gozo and Comino
- **Morning:** Embark on a boat voyage to the quiet island of Gozo, noted for its lovely towns, gorgeous scenery, and ancient attractions. Explore the defensive walls of the Cittadella, the island's capital, and meander through the small lanes dotted with classic Maltese dwellings.

- **Afternoon:** Venture to the quiet Ramla Bay, a lovely beach with golden sand and brilliant blue seas. Relax on the sun-kissed coastlines or enjoy a refreshing plunge in the Mediterranean Sea.

- **Evening:** Take a boat journey to the adjacent island of Comino, noted for its gorgeous Blue Lagoon, a natural marvel with crystal-clear waters and striking tints of blue and green. Enjoy a leisurely dip in the lagoon or relax on the sandy beach, surrounded by the calm of this picturesque island.

Day 3: Embracing the Natural Beauty of North Malta

- **Morning:** Discover the rugged beauty of Dingli Cliffs, the highest cliffs in Malta, affording stunning views of the Maltese shoreline and the Mediterranean Sea. Capture amazing panoramic images and admire the natural beauty of this wonderful environment.

- **Afternoon:** Explore the picturesque town of Mdina, Malta's old capital, and meander through its small alleyways adorned with Baroque architecture and historical attractions. Visit St. Paul's Cathedral, a beautiful landmark, and appreciate the panoramic views from the Mdina bastions.

- **Evening:** Conclude your Maltese adventure with a typical Maltese meal at a local restaurant, experiencing the tastes of the island's cuisine. Share tales and recollections of your Maltese travels while enjoying a great gastronomic experience.

One Week Itinerary

Day 1: Arrival and Settling In

- **Morning:** Arrive at Malta International Airport and check into your accommodation in Valletta, the island's lovely capital city.

- **Afternoon:** Take a leisurely walk around Valletta's old streets, admiring the architecture and soaking in the ambiance. Visit the Upper Barrakka Gardens for beautiful views of the Grand Harbour.

- **Evening:** Enjoy a typical Maltese supper at a local restaurant, relishing the tastes of the island's cuisine.

Day 2: Exploring Valletta and the Three Cities
- **Morning:** Immerse yourself in Valletta's rich history by visiting the St. John's Co-Cathedral, a marvel of Baroque architecture. Wander around the Grand Master's Palace, formerly the abode of Malta's rulers.

- **Afternoon:** Take a boat over the Grand Harbour to visit the Three Cities, a collection of walled cities with a particular appeal. Visit the Senglea Garden for panoramic views of the harbor.

- **Evening:** Experience the busy nightlife of St. Julian's, a popular center for pubs, clubs, and restaurants. Enjoy a dynamic supper with a view of Spinola Bay and immerse yourself in the bustling atmosphere of this seaside town.

Day 3: Unveiling the Hidden Gems of Gozo and Comino

- **Morning:** Embark on a boat voyage to the quiet island of Gozo, noted for its lovely towns, picturesque scenery, and ancient attractions. Explore the defensive walls of the Cittadella, the island's capital, and meander through the small lanes dotted with classic Maltese dwellings.

- **Afternoon:** Venture to the quiet Ramla Bay, a lovely beach with golden sand and brilliant blue waves. Relax on the sun-kissed coastlines or enjoy a refreshing plunge in the Mediterranean Sea.

- **Evening:** Take a boat journey to the adjacent island of Comino, noted for its gorgeous Blue Lagoon, a natural marvel with crystal-clear seas and striking tints of blue and green. Enjoy a leisurely dip in the lagoon or relax on the sandy beach, surrounded by the calm of this picturesque island.

Day 4: A Journey through Maltese History and Culture

- **Morning:** Visit the Malta National Museum in Valletta, delving into the island's rich history and cultural legacy. Explore the numerous displays portraying Malta's prehistoric, Roman, and medieval heritage.

- **Afternoon:** Immerse yourself in the ancient world at the Tarxien Temples, a UNESCO-listed landmark dating back to 3000 BC. Admire the megalithic buildings and envision the life of the people who created them.

- **Evening:** Experience a traditional Maltese folk music performance, enjoying the vibrant melodies and immersing yourself in the island's rich cultural heritage.

Day 5: Relaxing by the Sea and Exploring Natural Beauty

- **Morning:** Head to Golden Bay, a beautiful beach famed for its golden dunes and tranquil waves. Relax on the sun-kissed coastlines or enjoy a refreshing plunge in the Mediterranean Sea.

- **Afternoon:** Venture to the Dingli Cliffs, the highest cliffs in Malta, giving stunning views of the Maltese shoreline and the Mediterranean Sea. Capture amazing panoramic images and admire the natural beauty of this wonderful environment.

- **Evening:** Enjoy a relaxing evening at a beachside restaurant, eating excellent seafood dishes and viewing the sunset over the Mediterranean Sea.

Day 6: Unveiling the Charm of Mdina and Exploring the South

- **Morning:** Discover the picturesque village of Mdina, Malta's old capital, and meander through its small alleyways adorned with Baroque architecture and historical attractions. Visit St. Paul's Cathedral, a beautiful landmark, and appreciate the panoramic views from the Mdina bastions.

- **Afternoon:** Venture to the southern portion of Malta and visit the ancient temples of Hagar Qim and Mnajdra, UNESCO-listed ruins dating back to 3000 BC. Admire the megalithic buildings and acquire insights into the island's historic past.

- **Evening:** Indulge in a typical Maltese supper at a small restaurant in the south, relishing the flavors of the island's cuisine and experiencing the friendly hospitality.

Day 7: Departure and Bidding Farewell
- **Morning:** Enjoy a leisurely breakfast at your hotel and relish the closing moments of your Maltese journey.

- **Afternoon:** Take a cab or ride-sharing service to Malta International Airport for your departure.

- **Evening:** Depart from Malta, bringing with you fond memories of the island's rich history, lively culture, and spectacular natural beauty.

Cultural Exploration

Malta is a paradise for fans of cultural immersion. From its ancient temples and medieval defenses to its traditional festivals and active arts scene, Malta provides a rich tapestry of cultural experiences, encouraging tourists to go on a journey through the island's unique legacy and dynamic present.

Unearthing Malta's Ancient Treasures
Step back in time and dig into Malta's ancient history by touring the UNESCO-listed megalithic monuments of Hagar Qim and Mnajdra, dating back

to 3000 BC. These remarkable constructions, erected with large stone blocks, serve as testaments to the inventiveness and architectural ability of Malta's ancient people.

Wandering through Medieval Fortifications

Immerse yourself in the grandeur of Malta's medieval history by touring the walled towns of Valletta, Mdina, and Birgu. Valletta, Malta's capital city, is a UNESCO-listed jewel, filled with Baroque architecture, medieval fortifications, and the St. John's Co-Cathedral, a masterpiece of Baroque art. Mdina, Malta's historic capital, offers a timeless appeal with its tiny lanes lined with typical Maltese buildings and the majestic St. Paul's Cathedral. Birgu, one of the Three Cities, features a strong maritime heritage and breathtaking views of the Grand Harbour.

Celebrating Traditional Festivals

Experience the bright essence of Maltese culture by immersing yourself in the island's colorful festivities. The annual Festa di San Pawlu (Feast of St. Paul) in Valletta, celebrated in July, is a major event featuring fireworks, processions, and traditional Maltese music. The Notte Bianca (White Night) in Valletta, annually in September, turns the city into a midnight playground with live music, street performers, and lit streets.

Exploring Malta's Artistic Expressions

Discover the creative essence of Malta by experiencing its booming arts scene. Visit the MUZA - Museum of Fine Arts in Valletta, home to a collection of Maltese art from the 16th century to the current day. Immerse yourself in modern art at the St. James Cavalier Centre for Creativity in Valletta, a hub for exhibits, performances, and seminars.

Engaging with Local Customs and Traditions

Embrace the warmth and kindness of the Maltese people by participating in their local customs and traditions. Sample the island's exquisite gastronomy, eating traditional delicacies like fenek (rabbit stew) and pastizzi (savory pastries). Participate in a traditional Maltese ftira making workshop, learning to prepare this flatbread staple. Witness the talent of local artists by visiting the Malta National Crafts Centre in Ta' Qali, where you can observe traditional crafts including lacemaking, earthenware, and filigree.

Tips for a Culturally Immersive Adventure:
- **Embracing the Pace of Life:** Slow down and embrace the laid-back pace of life in Malta, relishing the moments and immersing yourself in the ambiance.

- **Learning a Few Maltese Phrases:** Learning simple Maltese words can increase your contacts with locals and express your appreciation for their culture.

- **Openness to Cultural Differences:** Embrace the variety of Maltese culture with an open mind and a readiness to explore new things.

Relaxation and Beach Time

Malta welcomes tourists seeking calm and renewal. With its beautiful beaches, isolated coves, and serene scenery, Malta provides a retreat for people looking to escape the rush and bustle of daily life and enjoy the calm of the Mediterranean.

Sun-Kissed Shores and Crystal-Clear Waters

Indulge in the ultimate beach vacation by heading to Golden Bay, a gorgeous beach on the northwest coast of Malta. Its golden dunes, crystal-clear seas, and moderate waves give the ideal backdrop for sunbathing, swimming, and water sports. For a more isolated experience, discover the secret coves of Ghajn Tuffieha Bay, where towering cliffs surround a quiet beach with turquoise waves.

A Serene Retreat on Comino

Embark on a boat voyage to the quiet island of Comino, a car-free haven noted for its magnificent Blue Lagoon. This natural beauty has crystal-clear seas, beautiful tints of blue and green, and a tranquil environment, making it a great site for swimming, snorkeling, or just sitting on the soft beaches.

Rejuvenating Spa Experiences

Pamper yourself with a refreshing spa session at one of Malta's luxury resorts or wellness facilities. Indulge in a choice of services, from massages and facials to hydrotherapy and aromatherapy, leaving you feeling refreshed and renewed.

Tranquil Getaways in Nature

Escape to the quiet countryside of Malta and discover hidden jewels like the Dingli Cliffs, the highest cliffs in Malta, affording stunning views of the Maltese shoreline and the Mediterranean Sea. Explore the calm Dingli woods, a refuge for nature enthusiasts, or meander through the tranquil grounds of the Verdala Palace, a 16th-century house surrounded by lush flora.

Savor Tranquil Moments

Embrace the laid-back pace of life in Malta and discover moments of solitude among the island's natural beauties. Enjoy a leisurely walk down the Sliema Promenade, appreciating the magnificent views of the Mediterranean Sea and the bustling ambiance of this coastal town. Relax on the sun-kissed sands of Ramla Bay, a lovely beach with golden sand and sparkling turquoise seas, or locate a hidden location on the cliffs overlooking the Blue Lagoon and immerse yourself in the calm of the surroundings.

Tips for a Relaxing Retreat:

- **Seek Out quiet Beaches:** Venture beyond the major tourist spots to uncover hidden coves and quiet beaches for a more serene experience.

- **Embrace the Tranquility:** Slow down and absorb the calm of Malta's natural beauty, relishing the moments and allowing the serene atmosphere to wash over you.

- **Indulge in Spa Treatments:** Pamper yourself with rejuvenating spa treatments to improve your relaxing experience.

- **Enjoy Leisurely dinners:** Savor the flavors of Maltese cuisine with leisurely dinners at coastal restaurants or traditional rural pubs.

- **Unplug and Disconnect:** Take a vacation from technology and immerse yourself in the present moment, allowing the peacefulness of Malta to revive your mind and soul.

Weekend Getaway

Picture yourself wandering through the sun-drenched streets of Valletta, Malta's enchanting capital city, enjoying the towering Baroque architecture and the panoramic vistas of the Grand Harbour. Imagine experiencing the pleasures of traditional Maltese food, a symphony of fresh flavors and culinary traditions. Envision yourself sunbathing on a pristine beach, the soft waves of the Mediterranean Sea lapping at the coast, while the sun paints the sky with colors of gold and red. This is Malta, a beautiful archipelago overflowing with history, culture, and natural beauty, providing a memorable weekend escape for discerning tourists.

Day 1: Unveiling Valletta's Timeless Charm

- **Morning:** Immerse yourself in the history and architecture of Valletta, a UNESCO-listed jewel. Explore the St. John's Co-Cathedral, a masterpiece of Baroque art, and see the delicate intricacies of its opulent interior.

- **Afternoon:** Wander through the Upper Barrakka Gardens, where stunning views of the Grand Harbour unroll before you. Witness the firing of the noon cannon, a centuries-old ceremony that resonates across the city.

- **Evening:** Savor a classic Maltese meal in a local restaurant, indulging in specialties like fenek (rabbit stew) or lampuki (local fish) followed by a glass of Maltese wine.

Day 2: Embracing the Islands' Natural Beauty

- **Morning:** Venture to the stunning Blue Lagoon on Comino, a car-free island haven. Relax on the silky white dunes, swim in the crystal-clear waters, or explore the adjacent caverns.

- **Afternoon:** Take a boat excursion to Gozo, Malta's sister island, noted for its calm charm and breathtaking vistas. Visit the Cittadella, Gozo's fortified city, and see the panoramic views from the bastions.

- **Evening:** Indulge in a traditional Maltese ftira making workshop, learning to prepare this flatbread staple and tasting your own gourmet masterpiece.

Day 3: A Cultural Tapestry of Traditions and Celebrations
- **Morning:** Immerse yourself in Malta's rich maritime legacy by visiting the Malta Maritime Museum in Birgu, one of the Three Cities. Explore exhibitions exhibiting the island's naval history and the effect of the water on Maltese culture.

- **Afternoon:** Witness the vivid energy of a typical Maltese festa, a festival of a patron saint. Enjoy the colorful processions, energetic music, and tasty food vendors that convert the streets into a joyous sanctuary.

- **Evening:** Conclude your Maltese excursion with a relaxing meal at a beachfront restaurant, eating excellent seafood dishes, and viewing the sunset over the Mediterranean Sea.

Tips for an Enchanting Weekend Getaway:

- Plan your itinerary in advance to make the most of your limited time.

- Consider hiring a vehicle to explore the islands at your own pace.

- Learn a few simple Maltese phrases to boost your contacts with locals.

- Be open to cultural differences and appreciate the distinctive charm of Malta.

- Savor the moments and build treasured memories of your Maltese adventure.

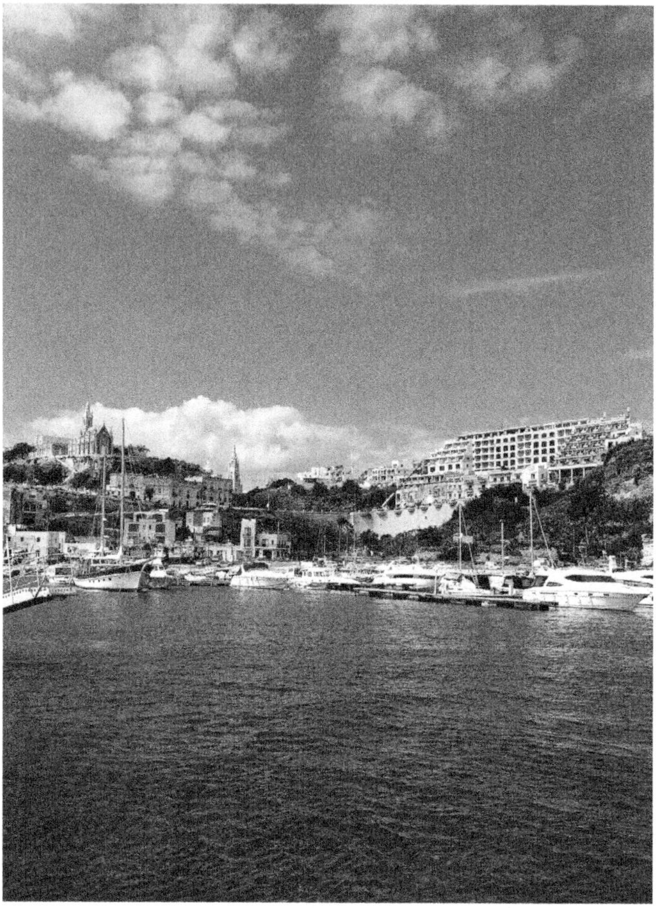

CHAPTER 9

Beaches

Malta is a dream for beach lovers. With its beautiful beaches, isolated coves, and calm coasts, Malta provides a symphony of sun-kissed sands, crystal-clear seas, and spectacular panoramas that will leave you craving for more.

Golden Bay: A Vibrant Beach Escape

Immerse yourself in the exuberant ambiance of Golden Bay, a famous beach on the northwest coast of Malta. Its golden beaches, calm waves, and a range of water sports facilities make it a great site for sunbathing, swimming, and enjoying a variety of activities.

Ghajn Tuffieha Bay: A Secluded Cove of Tranquility

Discover the hidden jewel of Ghajn Tuffieha Bay, a lovely cove flanked by high cliffs and giving a calm getaway from the rush and bustle. Relax on the sandy beaches, swim in the crystal-clear waters, or trek into the neighboring hills for beautiful vistas.

Blue Lagoon: An Enchanting Paradise of Crystal-Clear Waters

Venture to the stunning Blue Lagoon on Comino, a car-free island paradise. Its silky white beaches, crystal-clear blue seas, and surrounding caverns make a captivating backdrop for swimming, snorkeling, or just resting and enjoying the calm ambiance.

Ramla Bay: A Secluded Beach with Golden Sands

Unwind on the golden beaches of Ramla Bay, a lovely beach with brilliant turquoise seas and a laid-back environment. Relax on the sun-kissed coastlines, soak up the calm, or enjoy a refreshing plunge in the Mediterranean Sea.

Paradise Bay: A Picturesque Beach with Golden Sands

Escape to Paradise Bay, a quiet beach with golden sands and crystal-clear seas. Its secluded bay and calm environment make it a great site for sunbathing, swimming, and enjoying a relaxing retreat from the bustle.

Tips for an Enchanting Beach Escape:

- Plan your beach excursions according to the time of day to avoid crowds and enjoy the peace of the surroundings.

- Pack sunscreen, a hat, and sunglasses to protect yourself from the harsh Mediterranean sun.

- Bring your own food and beverages or select from the range of eateries and cafés available near the beaches.

- Respect the natural environment and leave no evidence of your presence.

- Embrace the peacefulness of Malta's beaches and create treasured moments among the island's coastline beauty.

Mellieħa Bay

Nestled in the scenic coastline of Mellieħa, Mellieħa Bay, also known as Għadira Bay, is a captivating place for families seeking a mix of leisure, adventure, and cultural immersion. With its gorgeous golden beaches, shallow crystal-clear seas, and a wealth of activities, Mellieħa Bay provides a place for treasured moments under the Maltese sun.

Unwind on the Golden Sands of Mellieħa Bay

Indulge in the ultimate beach vacation by heading to Mellieħa Bay, a stunning length of golden beaches spanning along the northeast coast of Malta. Its moderate waves, shallow seas, and decreasing depth make it a great site for families with small children, assuring them safety and happiness while splashing in the beautiful Mediterranean Sea.

Explore the Hidden Gems of Mellieħa Bay

Venture beyond the main beach area and discover the hidden wonders that Mellieħa Bay has to offer. Explore the picturesque beach of Armier Bay, noted for its snorkeling prospects, or travel to the isolated cove of Little Armier Bay, where you may avoid the tourists and enjoy the calm ambiance.

Experience a Thrilling Adventure in Popeye Village

Step into the beautiful world of Popeye Village, a unique theme park inspired by the renowned comic character. Explore the quaint sets, see the bright landscape, and enjoy a selection of activities, from boat excursions to live performances, making for an exciting family vacation.

Soak Up the Local Culture at Mellieħa's Historical Sites

Immerse yourself in Mellieħa's rich history by visiting the Mellieħa Parish Church, a stunning landmark overlooking the bay. Admire its Baroque architecture, discover its interior filled with elaborate carvings, and savor the panoramic views from the church's parvis.

Indulge in Culinary Delights at Seaside Restaurants

Savor the delights of Maltese cuisine by eating at one of Mellieħa Bay's numerous beachside restaurants. Enjoy fresh seafood delicacies, experience traditional Maltese specialties, and indulge in cool beverages while admiring the breathtaking views of the Mediterranean Sea.

Tips for an Enchanting Mellieħa Bay Adventure:

- Plan your vacation during the warmer months (May to October) to experience the greatest weather and beach conditions.

- Pack sunscreen, a hat, and sunglasses to protect yourself from the harsh Mediterranean sun.

- Consider hiring a vehicle to explore the local towns and attractions.

- Embrace the laid-back pace of life in Mellieħa and relish the times of relaxation and family fun.

- Create treasured memories by collecting images and writing your experiences.

Ramla Bay

Nestled on the northern coast of the calm island of Gozo, Ramla Bay, also known as Ramla l-Ħamra, is a charming paradise of golden dunes, crystal-clear seas, and a quiet environment. With its peculiar reddish-gold tone, this lovely beach provides a fascinating getaway from the masses, enabling tourists to engage in calm moments of relaxation and make treasured memories of Gozo's natural beauty.

Embracing the Tranquility of Ramla Bay's Golden Sands

Surrender to the calm of Ramla Bay, where soft golden sands extend along a secluded cove, giving a picture-perfect environment for sunbathing and enjoying the gentle caress of the Mediterranean Sea. The progressive depth of the waters makes it a great site for families with small children, enabling them to splash about safely while the sun paints the sky with colors of gold and scarlet.

Exploring the Hidden Gems of Ramla Bay

Venture beyond the main beach area and uncover the hidden wonders that Ramla Bay has to offer. Explore the neighboring cliffs, where you may discover hidden bays and rocky outcrops suitable for snorkeling or just enjoying the calm ambiance.

Hike into the neighboring valley, surrounded with classic Maltese farmhouses, and immerse yourself in the island's pastoral beauty.

Unveiling the Historical Significance of Ramla Bay

Delve into the rich history of Ramla Bay by exploring the surrounding ruins of Roman villas, and vestiges of a once-thriving Roman community. Imagine the life of people who previously inhabited these ancient buildings, their relationship to the land and the sea, and the legacy they left behind.

Savoring Local Delights at Ramla Bay's Seaside Cafés

Indulge in the tastes of Gozitan cuisine by eating at one of Ramla Bay's lovely beach cafés. Enjoy fresh seafood delicacies, experience traditional Maltese specialties, and indulge in cool beverages while admiring the breathtaking views of the Mediterranean Sea.

Embracing the Laid-Back Pace of Life at Ramla Bay

Slow down, relax, and experience the laid-back pace of life in Ramla Bay. Let the calm rhythm of the waves and the serene ambiance wash over you, providing moments of tranquility and refreshment. Savor the simple joys of life, from sunbathing and swimming to leisurely strolls down the beach, and build treasured memories among the beautiful beauty of Ramla Bay.

Tips for an Enchanting Ramla Bay Adventure:
- Plan your vacation during the warmer months (May to October) to experience the greatest weather and beach conditions.

- Pack sunscreen, a hat, and sunglasses to protect yourself from the harsh Mediterranean sun.

- Consider hiring a vehicle to explore the local towns and attractions on Gozo.

- Respect the natural environment and leave no evidence of your presence.

- Create treasured memories by collecting images and writing your experiences.

Paradise Bay

Nestled in the scenic coastline of Cirkewwa, Paradise Bay, also known as Ir-Ramla ta' Cirkewwa, is a captivating paradise of golden dunes, crystal-clear seas, and a tranquil ambiance. With its hidden position, immaculate natural beauty, and laid-back environment, Paradise Bay provides a fascinating retreat from the throng, encouraging tourists to enjoy calm moments of relaxation and make treasured memories among Malta's coastal treasures.

Embracing the Serenity of Paradise Bay's Golden Sands

Surrender to the calm of Paradise Bay, where soft golden sands extend along a hidden cove, giving a picture-perfect environment for sunbathing and enjoying the gentle caress of the Mediterranean Sea. The progressive depth of the waters makes it a great site for families with small children, enabling them to splash about safely while the sun paints the sky with colors of turquoise and blue.

Exploring the Hidden Gems of Paradise Bay
Venture beyond the main beach area and uncover the hidden wonders that Paradise Bay has to offer.

Explore the rocky outcrops around the cove, where you may discover hidden locations excellent for snorkeling or just enjoying the calm ambiance. Hike around the neighboring hills, where you may observe beautiful views of the Maltese coastline and the great Mediterranean Sea.

Unveiling the Natural Wonders of Paradise Bay
Delve into the natural beauty of Paradise Bay by exploring the neighboring caverns, where you may uncover secret ponds and unique rock formations. Admire the vivid marine life that inhabits these underwater havens, from colorful fish dashing among the corals to magnificent octopuses hiding in the shadows.

Savoring Local Delights at Paradise Bay's Seaside Kiosks
Indulge in the tastes of Maltese cuisine by eating at one of Paradise Bay's lovely beach kiosks. Enjoy fresh seafood delicacies, experience traditional Maltese specialties, and indulge in cool beverages

while admiring the breathtaking views of the Mediterranean Sea.

Embracing the Laid-Back Pace of Life in Paradise Bay

Slow down, relax, and experience the laid-back pace of life in Paradise Bay. Let the calm rhythm of the waves and the serene ambiance wash over you, providing moments of tranquility and refreshment. Savor the simple joys of life, from sunbathing and swimming to strolls down the beach, and build treasured memories among the beautiful beauty of Paradise Bay.

Tips for an Enchanting Paradise Bay Adventure:
- Plan your vacation during the warmer months (May to October) to experience the greatest weather and beach conditions.

- Pack sunscreen, a hat, and sunglasses to protect yourself from the harsh Mediterranean sun.

- Consider hiring a vehicle to explore the local towns and attractions in Malta.

- Respect the natural environment and leave no evidence of your presence.

- Create treasured memories by collecting images and writing your experiences.

Ghajn Tuffieha Bay

Nestled within the scenic shoreline of Malta's northwest coast, Ghajn Tuffieha Bay, also known as Tuffieħa Bay, is a mesmerizing refuge of golden dunes, crystal-clear blue seas, and a quiet ambiance. With its quiet position, immaculate natural beauty, and laid-back environment, Ghajn Tuffieha Bay provides a fascinating retreat from the throng, enabling tourists to indulge in calm moments of relaxation and make treasured memories among Malta's coastal treasures.

Embracing the Serenity of Ghajn Tuffieha Bay's Golden Sands

Surrender to the calm of Ghajn Tuffieha Bay, where soft golden sands run along a secluded cove, offering a picture-perfect environment for sunbathing and enjoying the gentle caress of the Mediterranean Sea. The progressive depth of the waters makes it a great site for families with small children, enabling them to splash about safely while the sun paints the sky with colors of turquoise and blue.

Exploring the Hidden Gems of Ghajn Tuffieha Bay

Venture beyond the main beach area and uncover the hidden wonders that Ghajn Tuffieha Bay has to offer. Explore the rocky outcrops around the cove, where you may discover hidden locations excellent for snorkeling or just enjoying the calm ambiance. Hike around the neighboring hills, where you may observe beautiful views of the Maltese coastline and the great Mediterranean Sea.

Unveiling the Natural Wonders of Ghajn Tuffieha Bay

Delve into the natural beauty of Ghajn Tuffieha Bay by exploring the adjacent caverns, where you may uncover secret pools and interesting rock formations. Admire the vivid marine life that inhabits these underwater havens, from colorful fish dashing among the corals to magnificent octopuses hiding in the shadows.

Savoring Local Delights at Ghajn Tuffieha Bay's Seaside Restaurants

Indulge in the delicacies of Maltese cuisine by eating at one of Ghajn Tuffieha Bay's picturesque beachside eateries. Enjoy fresh seafood delicacies, experience traditional Maltese specialties, and indulge in cool beverages while admiring the breathtaking views of the Mediterranean Sea.

Embracing the Laid-Back Pace of Life at Ghajn Tuffieha Bay

Slow down, relax, and experience the laid-back pace of life in Ghajn Tuffieha Bay. Let the calm rhythm of the waves and the serene ambiance wash over you, providing moments of tranquility and refreshment. Savor the simple joys of life, from sunbathing and swimming to strolls down the beach, and build treasured memories among the beautiful beauty of Ghajn Tuffieha Bay.

Tips for an Enchanting Ghajn Tuffieha Bay Adventure:

- Plan your vacation during the warmer months (May to October) to experience the greatest weather and beach conditions.

- Pack sunscreen, a hat, and sunglasses to protect yourself from the harsh Mediterranean sun.

- Consider hiring a vehicle to explore the local towns and attractions in Malta.

- Respect the natural environment and leave no evidence of your presence.

- Create treasured memories by shooting images and writing your experiences.

Additional Enchanting Experiences at Ghajn Tuffieha Bay:

- Embark on a boat trip: Explore the coastline from a fresh viewpoint and find secret coves and isolated areas.

- Enjoy a picnic by the sea: Pack a wonderful picnic basket and enjoy a leisurely dinner in the quiet surroundings.

- Try your hand at water sports: Engage in a variety of activities, from kayaking and paddleboarding to snorkeling and scuba diving.

- Watch the sunset over the Mediterranean Sea: Capture the stunning sight of the sun painting the sky with shades of gold and scarlet.

- Embrace the beauty and quiet of Ghajn Tuffieha Bay and create unique moments among the lovely landscapes of Malta.

Riviera Beach

Nestled within the craggy terrain of Malta's north coast, Riviera Beach, also known as Ir-Ramla tal-Mixquqa, is a beautiful oasis of crystal-clear blue seas, golden beaches, and a quiet environment. With its isolated position, immaculate natural beauty, and laid-back environment, Riviera Beach provides a fascinating retreat from the throng, enabling guests to indulge in calm moments of relaxation and make treasured memories among Malta's coastal treasures.

Surrender to the Tranquility of Riviera Beach's Golden Sands

Step onto the smooth golden sands of Riviera Beach and feel the soothing caress of the Mediterranean Sea under your feet. Allow the soothing beat of the waves to wash over you as you drink up the sun's warmth and immerse yourself in the quiet ambiance. This quiet cove, set between towering cliffs, provides a refuge of peace and calm, distant from the rush and bustle of daily life.

Explore the Hidden Gems of Riviera Beach

Venturing beyond the main beach area, you'll find the hidden wonders that Riviera Beach has to offer. Explore the rocky outcrops around the cove, where you may discover hidden locations excellent for snorkeling or just enjoying the calm ambiance. Climb the neighboring cliffs, where you may appreciate amazing views of the Maltese coastline and the broad Mediterranean Sea.

Unveil the Underwater Wonders of Riviera Beach

Delve into the abundant aquatic life that inhabits the crystal-clear waters of Riviera Beach. With its rich marine life, this undersea paradise is great for snorkeling and scuba diving. Discover a rainbow of colorful fish dashing among the corals, see gigantic octopus hiding in the shadows, and discover the splendor of the underwater world that lies under the surface.

Savor Local Delights at Riviera Beach's Charming Restaurant

Indulge in the tastes of Maltese cuisine by eating at the beautiful restaurant situated only feet from the beach. Enjoy fresh seafood delicacies, experience traditional Maltese specialties, and indulge in cool beverages while admiring the breathtaking views of the Mediterranean Sea.

Embrace the Laid-Back Pace of Life at Riviera Beach

Slow down, relax, and experience the laid-back pace of life at Riviera Beach. Let the calm rhythm of the waves and the serene ambiance wash over you, providing moments of tranquility and refreshment. Savor the simple joys of life, from sunbathing and swimming to leisurely strolls down the beach, and build treasured memories among the beautiful beauty of Riviera Beach.

Tips for an Enchanting Riviera Beach Adventure:

- Plan your vacation during the warmer months (May to October) to experience the greatest weather and beach conditions.

- Pack sunscreen, a hat, and sunglasses to protect yourself from the harsh Mediterranean sun.

- Consider hiring a vehicle to explore the local towns and attractions in Malta.

- Respect the natural environment and leave no evidence of your presence.

- Create treasured memories by shooting images and writing your experiences.

Additional Enchanting Experiences at Riviera Beach:

- Embark on a boat trip: Explore the coastline from a fresh viewpoint and find secret coves and isolated areas.

- Enjoy a picnic by the sea: Pack a wonderful picnic basket and enjoy a leisurely dinner in the quiet surroundings.

- Try your hand at water sports: Engage in a variety of activities, from kayaking and paddleboarding to snorkeling and scuba diving.

- Watch the sunset over the Mediterranean Sea: Capture the stunning sight of the sun painting the sky with shades of gold and scarlet.

- Embrace the beauty and quiet of Riviera Beach and create unique experiences among the lovely landscapes of Malta.

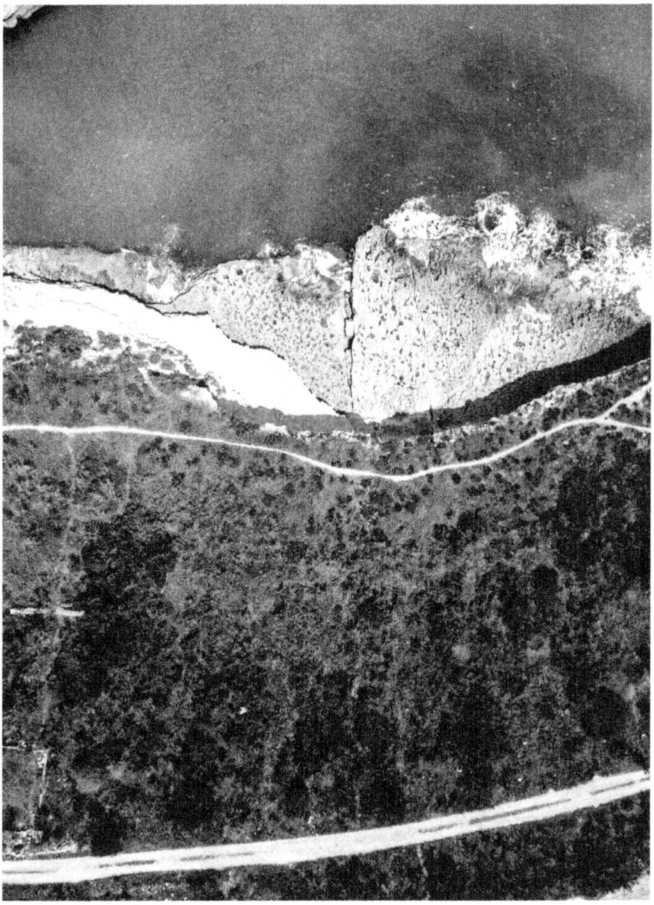

CHAPTER 10

Outdoor Activities

Malta, provides a plethora of outdoor activities to suit all interests and inclinations. From exploring craggy cliffs and quiet coves to indulging in adrenaline-pumping water sports and uncovering hidden historical jewels, Malta's landscapes and rich cultural history offer a wonderful background for adventure and discovery.

Embrace the Thrills of Water Sports
- **Scuba Diving and Snorkeling:** Immerse yourself in the underwater world of Malta's crystal-clear waters and experience a kaleidoscope of marine life. Explore submerged shipwrecks, swim among colorful fish, and marvel at the vivid coral reefs that teem with life.

- **Kayaking and Paddleboarding:** Glide over the peaceful seas of Malta's bays and coves, enjoying the serenity of the surroundings and appreciating the spectacular coastal panorama. Explore secret caverns, paddle along isolated sections of shoreline, and feel the excitement of exploring the Mediterranean Sea from a new viewpoint.

- **Windsurfing and Kitesurfing:** Harness the force of the wind and push yourself with amazing windsurfing and kitesurfing activities. Catch the perfect wave, feel the adrenaline rush, and enjoy the excitement of gliding over the water's surface.

Venture into Malta's Enchanting Hiking Trails
- **Dingli Cliffs:** Scale the heights of the Dingli Cliffs, the highest cliffs in Malta, and marvel at the panoramic views of the Maltese shoreline and the Mediterranean Sea. Capture amazing images, admire the raw

beauty of this natural treasure, and feel the exhilaration of reaching the peak.

- **Mnajdra and Mistra Valleys:** Embark on a picturesque trek through the Mnajdra and Mistra Valleys, a sanctuary of natural beauty and historical value. Admire the green farmlands, examine the remnants of old temples, and snap magnificent images of the surrounding landscape.

- **Verdala Palace Gardens:** Wander around the tranquil grounds of Verdala Palace, a 16th-century house surrounded by beautiful flora. Enjoy a leisurely walk around the fountains, sculptures, and groomed lawns, or uncover the secret bird refuge inside the grounds.

Uncover Malta's Hidden Gems by Cycling

- **Coastal Cycle Routes:** Embark on a picturesque cycling excursion around

Malta's coastal bike paths, experiencing the stunning views of the Mediterranean Sea and the surrounding surroundings. Explore lovely towns, explore secret coves, and feel the excitement of exploring the island's various landscapes.

- **Inland Cycling Routes:** Venture into the heart of Malta's countryside and visit its rural communities, traditional farms, and hidden historical jewels. Cycle through quiet valleys, face hard peaks and discover the real beauty of Malta's off-the-beaten-path terrain.

- **Mountain Biking Trails:** Challenge yourself with exciting mountain bike paths that meander across Malta's mountainous landscape. Conquer steep slopes, uncover secret routes, and enjoy the thrill of adrenaline-pumping rides in the stunning natural environment.

Experience Malta's Cultural Heritage

- **Explore Ancient Temples:** Delve into Malta's rich history by touring the awe-inspiring ancient temples at Hagar Qim, Mnajdra, and Tarxien. Admire the elaborate carvings, the opulent interior covered with gold leaf, and the spectacular Caravaggio masterpiece, "The Beheading of St. John the Baptist."

- **Visit Historical Fortifications:** Step back in time and explore around the majestic walls of Valletta, Malta's capital city. Explore the St. John's Co-Cathedral, a masterpiece of Baroque art, and marvel at the panoramic views from the Upper Barrakka Gardens.

- **Discover Malta's Maritime Heritage:** Immerse yourself in Malta's maritime heritage at the Malta Maritime Museum in

Birgu. Explore exhibitions showing historic ships and relics, acquire insights into the island's participation in naval wars, and comprehend the significance of the sea to Maltese culture.

Embrace the Tranquility of Nature
- **Relax on Pristine Beaches:** Indulge in the ideal beach vacation by heading to Malta's exquisite beaches, such as Golden Bay, Ghajn Tuffieha Bay, and Blue Lagoon. Unwind on the soft beaches, swim in the crystal-clear waters, and enjoy the quiet ambiance among stunning coastline views.

- **Explore Enchanting Caves:** Discover Malta's hidden jewels by visiting its fascinating caverns, such as the Blue Grotto and the Wied il-Għajn Cave. Witness the beautiful interaction of light and water, enjoy the distinctive rock formations, and feel the calm of these hidden natural beauties.

- **Enjoy Scenic Boat Trips:** Embark on a picturesque boat tour and experience Malta's shoreline from a fresh viewpoint. Discover quiet coves, enjoy the towering cliffs, and

Water Sports and Diving

Malta, provides a variety of water sports and diving options to suit all levels of expertise and thrill-seeking interests. From exploring the crystal-clear depths of the Mediterranean to engaging in adrenaline-pumping water sports,

Malta's broad choice of activities offers a fascinating retreat for anyone seeking an active and adventurous holiday.

Embark on an Underwater Adventure with Diving and Snorkeling

- **Discover a Kaleidoscope of Marine Life:** Immerse yourself in the underwater world of Malta's crystal-clear waters and experience a kaleidoscope of marine life. Explore submerged shipwrecks, swim among colorful fish, and marvel at the vivid coral reefs that teem with life.

- **Scuba Diving for Beginners and Experienced Divers:** Whether you're a seasoned scuba diver or a curious novice, Malta's dive spots cater to all levels of expertise. Explore shallow reefs bursting with life, journey into deeper seas for more demanding dives, or even experience the excitement of night diving.

- **Snorkeling in Secluded Coves and Bays:** Embark on a snorkeling expedition and explore the hidden beauty of Malta's secret coves and beaches. Explore the underwater world with ease, observe the vivid marine life, and experience the calm of the surrounding surroundings.

Indulge in Exhilarating Water Sports
- **Catch the Perfect Wave with Windsurfing and Kitesurfing:** Harness the force of the wind and push yourself with amazing windsurfing and kitesurfing activities. Catch the perfect wave, feel the adrenaline rush, and enjoy the pleasure of gliding over the water's surface.

- **Explore Hidden Coves with Kayaking and Paddleboarding:** Glide over the peaceful seas of Malta's bays and coves, enjoying the serenity of the surroundings and appreciating the spectacular coastal panorama. Explore secret caverns, paddle along isolated sections of shoreline, and feel the excitement of exploring the Mediterranean Sea from a new viewpoint.

- **Ride the Waves with Jet Skis and Parasailing:** Experience the excitement of riding the waves at high speeds on a jet ski, or flying through the air while parasailing and seeing the breathtaking views of Malta's coastline from above.

Experience the Unique Thrills of Malta's Water Sports

- **Flyboarding:** Elevate your water sports experience to new heights with flyboarding. Propel yourself into the air with a forceful jet of water, execute aerial acrobatics, and feel the sensation of flying.

- **Seabreeze Cruises:** Embark on a magnificent Seabreeze cruise and experience a day of leisure and adventure. Explore secret coves, indulge in wonderful cuisine and beverages, and enjoy the calm of the Mediterranean Sea.

- **Banana Boating and Ringo Rides:** Experience the thrill and excitement of banana boating and ringo rides. Hold on tight as you're tugged along at tremendous speeds, laughing and enjoying the excitement of the ride.

Safety Tips for Water Sports and Diving in Malta

- Always pick a trustworthy and experienced water sports and diving operator.

- Follow the directions and safety recommendations supplied by your instructor or guide.

- Be alert of your surroundings and your fellow participants.

- Use proper safety gear, including life jackets or buoyancy aids as necessary.

- Respect the aquatic ecosystem and leave no evidence of your presence.

embark on an incredible water sports and diving trip in Malta and make treasured moments among the bright sceneries and crystal-clear seas of this Mediterranean paradise.

Hiking and Nature Trails

Malta, provides a variety of hiking and nature routes to suit all levels of expertise and fitness. From exploring craggy cliffs and quiet coves to crossing green valleys and uncovering hidden historical jewels, Malta's broad assortment of trails offers a gorgeous and fascinating retreat for anyone seeking an active and adventurous holiday.

Embark on Scenic Coastal Hikes
- **Dingli Cliffs Walk:** Ascend the Dingli Cliffs, the highest cliffs in Malta, and marvel at the stunning panoramic views of the Maltese shoreline and the Mediterranean Sea. Capture amazing images, admire the raw beauty of this natural treasure, and feel the exhilaration of reaching the peak.

- **Xlendi Walk:** Venture into the lovely Xlendi Valley and start on a magnificent stroll along the shoreline. Admire the rich flora, explore secret caverns, and find the quiet Xlendi Bay, a paradise of golden dunes and crystal-clear seas.

- **Ramla Bay Walk:** Embark on a leisurely stroll from Ramla Bay, a lovely cove with reddish-gold beaches, and uncover the hidden beauties of the region. Explore the neighboring hills, see the classic Maltese farmhouses, and catch breathtaking views of the Mediterranean Sea.

Venture into Malta's Enchanting Inland Trails

- **Majjistral Nature and History Park:** Immerse yourself in the rich flora and animals of the Majjistral Nature and History Park, a refuge of natural beauty and historical value. Explore historic cart ruts, find Punic graves, and appreciate the calm of the surrounding countryside.

- **Verdala Palace Gardens:** Wander around the tranquil grounds of Verdala Palace, a 16th-century house surrounded by beautiful flora. Enjoy a leisurely walk around the fountains, sculptures, and groomed lawns, or uncover the secret bird refuge inside the grounds.

- **Buskett Gardens:** Escape the rush and bustle of daily life and find comfort in the quiet Buskett Gardens, a wide stretch of woods known as Malta's "lungs." Stroll along shaded trails, see the towering trees, and have a picnic in the calm surroundings.

Embrace the Challenge of Malta's Hilly Trails

- **Mnajdra and Mistra Valleys Walk:** Embark on a tough journey through the Mnajdra and Mistra Valleys, a sanctuary of natural beauty and historical value. Ascend high slopes, view the green farmlands, and discover the remnants of old temples.

- **Marfa Ridge Walk:** Challenge yourself with the Marfa Ridge Walk, a tough walk that rewards beautiful vistas. Conquer difficult ascents, enjoy panoramic panoramas of Malta's northern shore, and find hidden natural sites.

- **Victoria Lines Walk:** Step back in time and follow the Victoria Lines, a defensive fortification system created in the 19th century. Hike up the ridge, examine the reconstructed forts, and understand the historical importance of this military monument.

Discover Hidden Gems and Enchanting Landscapes

- **Wied il-Għajn Walk**: Embark on a leisurely trek through the Wied il-Għajn Valley, noted for its lush flora and natural springs. Discover secret waterfalls, explore the nearby caverns, and enjoy the calm of the valley's quiet ambiance.

- **Il-Maqluba Walk:** Delve into the peculiar geology of Malta by following the Il-Maqluba Walk, a route that leads to a collapsed geological feature known as the "fault trough." Admire the rock formations, explore the surrounding countryside, and enjoy the raw beauty of the natural surroundings.

- **Golden Bay to Ġnejna Bay Walk:** Embark on a magnificent coastal stroll from Golden Bay, a famous beach with golden sands, to Ġnejna Bay, a quiet cove famed for its calm. Enjoy spectacular views of the Mediterranean Sea, explore secret coves, and enjoy in a refreshing dip at the conclusion of your journey.

Safety Tips for Hiking in Malta
- Always arrange your trek according to your fitness level and experience.

- Choose proper footwear and clothes for the terrain and weather conditions.

- Carry lots of water and food to remain hydrated and energized.

- Be careful of your surroundings and any risks, such as steep cliffs and uneven terrain.

- Respect the natural environment and leave no evidence of your presence.

Embrace the beauty and peacefulness of Malta's hiking paths and create treasured moments among the island's various landscapes and fascinating natural wonders.

Boat Trips and Excursions

Malta, an archipelago of beautiful islands situated among the turquoise seas of the Mediterranean Sea, provides a variety of boat cruises and excursions to suit all tastes and inclinations. From exploring secret coves and quiet beaches to traveling along the mountainous coastline and uncovering hidden historical jewels, Malta's broad choice of boat excursions offers a fascinating and enlightening retreat for anyone wanting an energetic and adventurous holiday.

Embark on a Scenic Cruise along Malta's Coastline

- **Comino and the Blue Lagoon:** Venture to the picturesque island of Comino and explore the lovely Blue Lagoon, a refuge of crystal-clear turquoise seas and silky white dunes. Explore the neighboring caverns, swim in the peaceful waters, and engage in a leisurely day among the amazing natural beauty.

- **Gozo and Dwejra Bay:** Embark on a picturesque trip to Gozo, Malta's second-largest island, and see the delights of Dwejra Bay, home to the renowned Inland Sea and the Azure Window, a natural limestone arch that collapsed in 2017. Explore secret tunnels, marvel at the geological formations, and make treasured moments among the island's stunning surroundings.

- **Valletta Harbour Cruise:** Immerse yourself in the rich history of Malta's capital city by going on a Valletta Harbour Cruise. Admire the majestic walls, uncover secret nooks of the city, and snap breathtaking images of the Grand Harbour.

Explore Malta's Hidden Coves and Secluded Beaches

- Blue Lagoon and Caves Cruise: Set sail on an exciting voyage to the Blue Lagoon, a refuge of crystal-clear turquoise seas and silky white dunes. Explore the neighboring caverns, swim in the peaceful waters, and have a fun-filled day of snorkeling and diving among the abundant marine life.

- **Crystal Lagoon and Comino Caves Cruise:** Venture to the Crystal Lagoon, a hidden jewel of Comino, and explore its astoundingly beautiful waters. Explore the neighboring caverns, observe the unusual rock formations, and enjoy a quiet day of swimming and sunbathing.

- **Santa Maria Bay and Mgarr ix-Xini Bay Cruise:** Embark on a picturesque trip around Malta's coastline and explore the isolated Santa Maria Bay and Mgarr ix-Xini Bay. Enjoy a refreshing plunge in the crystal-clear waters, indulge in great local food, and absorb the calm of these hidden jewels.

Experience the Thrill of Speedboat Adventures
- **Comino and Gozo Speedboat Adventure:** Embark on an adventurous speedboat excursion to Comino and Gozo, discovering secret coves, swimming in private lagoons, and experiencing the thrill of high-speed rides. Discover the beauty of the Maltese islands from a fresh viewpoint and create amazing memories.

- **Malta Coastline Speedboat Tour:** Experience the excitement of a high-speed boat trip around Malta's rough coastline, passing past prominent monuments and finding secret coves. Enjoy the adrenaline thrill, shoot breathtaking images, and enjoy the beauty of Malta from a new viewpoint.

Indulge in Luxurious Yacht Charters and Private Excursions

- **Private Yacht Charter:** Charter a magnificent boat and explore Malta's shoreline in style. Enjoy individualized treatment, indulge in exquisite food, and design bespoke itineraries to fit your interests.

- **Private Comino and Blue Lagoon Excursion:** Embark on a private journey to Comino and the Blue Lagoon, gaining exclusive access to this lovely sanctuary. Swim in the crystal-clear waters, explore the neighboring caverns, and make treasured moments in the calm of this secluded paradise.

- **Sunset Cruise with Dinner and Champagne:** Experience the romance of a sunset sail over the Mediterranean Sea, accompanied by a scrumptious supper and cool champagne. Admire the spectacular sights as the sun paints the sky with shades of orange and purple, creating a romantic and unique experience.

Safety Tips for Boat Trips and Excursions in Malta

- Always pick a trustworthy and competent boat excursion operator.

- Follow the directions and safety requirements supplied by your team members.

- Be alert of your surroundings and any risks, such as strong currents and sudden weather changes.

- Use proper safety gear, such as life jackets, as necessary.

- Respect the aquatic ecosystem and leave no evidence of your presence.

Embrace the beauty and peacefulness of Malta's boat tours and excursions and build treasured moments among the island's various landscapes and fascinating coastline treasures.

303

CHAPTER 11

Shopping In Malta

Malta, provides an abundance of shopping choices to suit all tastes and budgets. From visiting lively markets and quaint shops to finding unique handicrafts and traditional Maltese items, Malta's varied shopping scene offers a wonderful and rewarding experience for anyone wishing to immerse themselves in the island's culture and customs.

Embrace the Fashion and Lifestyle Finds

- **High-Street Brands and Designer Boutiques:** Explore the stylish streets of Valletta and Sliema, where you'll discover a mix of international high-street brands and designer shops. Discover the newest trends, engage in shopping therapy, and make fashionable additions to your wardrobe.

- **Local Fashion and Artisan Designs:** Support local talent and discover unique fashion treasures at independent retailers and artisan studios. Admire the beautiful patterns, handmade items, and the creative spirit of Maltese fashion.

- **Homeware and Lifestyle Stores:** Enhance your home décor and find unique lifestyle goods at Malta's attractive homeware and lifestyle boutiques. Browse through a chosen assortment of handmade ceramics, traditional Maltese tiles, and local design elements.

Tips for a Memorable Shopping Experience in Malta

- Plan your shopping visits according to the operating hours of local markets and shops.

- Embrace the negotiating culture, particularly in local markets and souvenir shops.

- Be careful of the local currency, the euro, and bring adequate cash for your shopping endeavors.

- Respect the local customs and traditions, and be mindful of other shoppers.

- Create treasured memories by collecting images and writing your shopping adventures.

Embark on a fun shopping spree in Malta and uncover a treasure trove of local items, traditional handicrafts, and unique fashion discoveries that represent the island's rich legacy and lively culture.

Traditional Crafts and Souvenirs

Malta, provides a wealth of traditional crafts and souvenirs to suit all tastes and budgets. From delicate lacework and handmade ceramics to distinctive glasswork and silver jewelry, Malta's rich past and creative traditions are represented in the broad variety of handcrafted treasures that await discovery.

Discover the Exquisite Beauty of Maltese Lace
- **Filfla:** Admire the delicate beauty of Filfla, a traditional Maltese lacemaking method that combines precise needlework and a variety of stitching designs. Discover delicate lace doilies, scarves, and tablecloths, each a monument to the skill and craftsmanship of Maltese lacemakers.

- **Tombolo:** Immerse yourself in the world of Tombolo, a kind of lacemaking that employs a wooden cushion and bobbins to create beautiful patterns. Discover gorgeous lace collars, handkerchiefs, and ornamental items that display the accuracy and creativity of this ancient trade.

- **Traditional Lacemaking Workshops:** Witness the enchantment of traditional lacemaking firsthand by visiting one of Malta's lacemaking workshops. Observe the talented craftsmen at work, learn about the history and methods of Maltese lacemaking, and maybe even try your hand at crafting this delicate art form.

Treasure the Authenticity of Handmade Pottery

- **Maltese Pottery:** Discover the rich legacy of Maltese pottery, defined by its unusual forms, brilliant colors, and detailed decorations. Admire handmade vases, bowls, and plates, each a monument to the skill and beauty of Maltese potters.

- **The Mdina Pottery:** Explore the Mdina Pottery, a famous pottery factory noted for its manufacture of traditional Maltese ceramics. Discover a broad assortment of handmade ceramic items, from bright tiles and artistic figures to functional cookware and tableware.

- **Local Pottery Markets:** Immerse yourself in the colorful ambiance of local ceramic markets and uncover a treasure trove of handmade pottery objects. Browse through booths packed with unique objects, each exhibiting the ingenuity and skill of Maltese craftsmen.

Embrace the Beauty of Maltese Glasswork

- **Maltese Glassblowing:** Witness the amazing technique of Maltese glassblowing, where molten glass is turned into beautiful patterns and vivid decorations. Discover a collection of artisan glasswork, from beautiful vases and bowls to delicate jewelry pieces.

- **Mdina Glass:** Explore Mdina Glass, a famous glassblowing studio noted for its manufacture of high-quality glasswork. Admire a range of handmade glass creations, each showing the skill and accuracy of Maltese glassblowers.

- **Glassblowing Demonstrations:** Experience the excitement of seeing a live glassblowing demonstration and observe firsthand the expertise and creativity involved in this traditional trade. Observe the metamorphosis of molten glass into stunning pieces, and acquire a greater understanding of the talent of Maltese glassblowers.

Admire the Elegance of Silver Jewelry
- **Filigree Silverwork:** Discover the complex beauty of Maltese filigree silverwork, a

delicate technique that requires twisting and weaving tiny silver threads into ornate shapes. Admire handmade silver earrings, necklaces, and bracelets, each a monument to the skill and craftsmanship of Maltese silversmiths.

- **Traditional Maltese Jewelry Designs:** Immerse yourself in the rich legacy of Maltese jewelry creation, defined by its distinctive themes, symbolism, and delicate workmanship. Discover a collection of handmade jewelry items, from tiny pendants and rings to striking necklaces and bracelets.

- **Local Jewelry Artisans:** Support local jewelry artists by visiting their workshops and retailers. Discover a range of unique and individual jewelry items, each exhibiting the ingenuity and skill of Maltese silversmiths.

Tips for Finding Traditional Crafts and Souvenirs in Malta

- Explore local markets and artisan festivals, such as the Sunday Market in Valletta and the Crafts Village in Ta' Qali.

- Visit traditional workshops and artisan studios to observe the artistic process firsthand.

- Support local artists by buying directly from them, guaranteeing fair pricing and ethical practices.

- Haggle nicely in local markets and souvenir stores to get the best deals.

- Create treasured memories by collecting images and writing your shopping adventures.

Embrace the rich historical and cultural traditions of Malta by experiencing the exquisite beauty of traditional crafts and souvenirs. From delicate lacework and handcrafted ceramics to complex glasswork and beautiful silver jewelry, each item displays the skill, creativity, and love of Maltese artists.

Local Markets and Shopping Districts

Malta, provides a lovely combination of traditional markets and contemporary retail areas to suit all interests and budgets. From exploring bustling markets filled with local produce and handcrafted treasures to wandering through charming streets lined with boutiques and designer stores, Malta's diverse shopping scene provides a vibrant and enriching experience for those seeking to immerse themselves in the island's culture and traditions.

Delve into the Heart of Valletta's Shopping Scene

- **The Sunday Market:** Join the exciting atmosphere of the Sunday Market in Valletta, held every Sunday morning at Ordnance Street. Discover a treasure trove of local products, handicrafts, souvenirs, and antiques, all at affordable rates.

- **Merchants Street:** Wander along the picturesque Merchants Street, a pedestrian-only zone packed with small boutiques, artisan crafts, and typical Maltese souvenir stores. Uncover unique handicrafts, local delicacies, and one-of-a-kind treasures among the small lanes and old-world charm.

- **Republic Street:** Stroll down Republic Street, Valletta's main street, and find a colorful mix of shops, boutiques, and department stores. Admire the exquisite architecture, browse through the varied assortment of items, and absorb the bustling atmosphere of the city's retail core.

Explore the Thrill of Local Markets and Fairs

- **The Birgu Market:** Venture to the Birgu Market, a historic Maltese market famed for its genuine atmosphere and numerous wares. Browse among booths full of fresh fruits and vegetables, spices and herbs, home products, and local delicacies.

- **The Marsaxlokk Fish Market:** Experience the bustling atmosphere of the Marsaxlokk Fish Market, held every Sunday morning. Admire the colorful display of fresh seafood, participate in active haggling with the fishermen, and observe the true Maltese way of life.

- **The Crafts Village at Ta' Qali:** Immerse yourself in the world of traditional Maltese crafts in the Crafts Village at Ta' Qali, a dynamic center of craftsmen and workshops. Discover handcrafted ceramics, complex lacework, gorgeous silver jewelry, and unique gifts that represent the island's rich past.

Discover Culinary Delights and Traditional Fare

- **The Valletta Food Market:** Embark on a gastronomic experience at the Valletta Food Market, a sanctuary for foodies and those seeking traditional Maltese cuisine. Sample local cheeses, delight in freshly made bread, and relish the scents of traditional Maltese food.

- **Local Delicacies and Confectioneries:** Indulge in the delicious pleasures of Malta's traditional confectioneries, such as the famed honey rings (imqaret) and the nougat-like halva. Discover local specialties like the pastizzi, savory pastries filled with ricotta cheese or peas, and the ftira, a classic Maltese flatbread topped with different fillings.

Venture into Malta's Shopping Districts

- **Sliema's Shopping Hub:** Explore the busy retail area of Sliema, where you'll discover a mix of high-street brands, local shops, and souvenir stores. Discover the newest trends, engage in retail therapy, and enjoy the vibrant ambiance of this renowned shopping location.

- **St. Julian's Shopping Scene:** Immerse yourself in the contemporary retail environment of St. Julian's, recognized for its combination of fashion shops, designer stores, and entertainment alternatives. Discover unusual and fashionable goods, enjoy the upmarket ambiance, and soak up the dynamic energy of this renowned nightlife location.

- **Victoria's Shopping Charm:** Venture to Victoria, the city of Gozo, and find a delightful shopping area packed with local boutiques, traditional craft shops, and souvenir stores. Admire the island's distinctive workmanship, browse through a range of handcrafted things, and experience the real Gozitan ambiance.

Tips for Navigating Local Markets and Shopping Districts in Malta

- Plan your shopping visits according to the operating hours of local markets and shops.

- Embrace the negotiating culture, particularly in local markets and souvenir shops.

- Be careful of the local currency, the euro, and bring adequate cash for your shopping endeavors.

- Respect the local customs and traditions, and be mindful of other shoppers.

- Create treasured memories by collecting images and writing your shopping adventures.

Embark on a fascinating excursion around Malta's local markets and shopping areas and uncover a treasure trove of local items, traditional handicrafts, and unique fashion discoveries. From crowded markets brimming with bright energy to lovely alleyways lined with shops, Malta's unique retail scene gives an exceptional experience that reflects the island's rich tradition and dynamic culture.

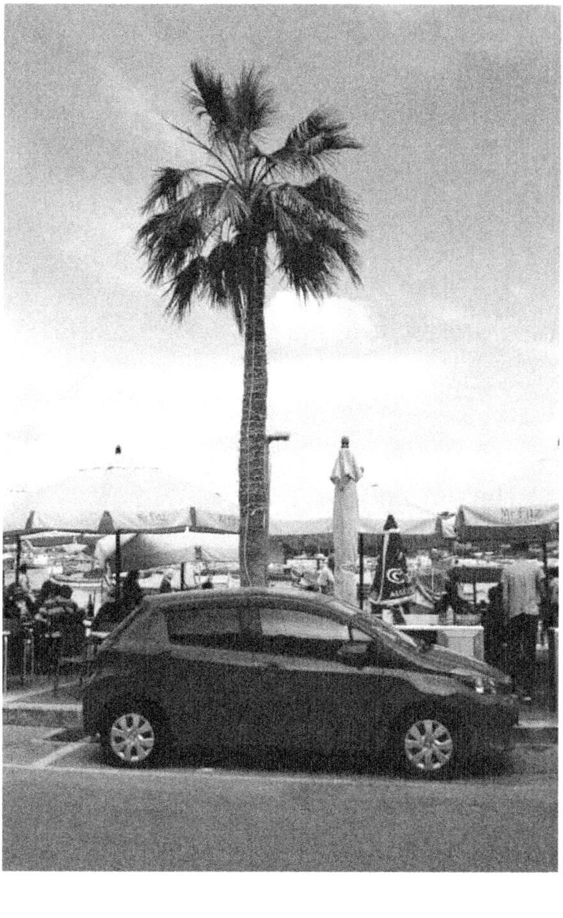

CHAPTER 12

Nightlife and Entertainment

Malta, provides a plethora of nightlife and entertainment alternatives to suit all tastes and inclinations. From throbbing dance clubs and bustling pubs to traditional music venues and open-air theatres, Malta's thriving nightlife scene delivers a wonderful and engaging experience for anyone wishing to immerse themselves in the island's culture and customs.

Experience the Energy of Paceville, Malta's Party Hub

- **Havana Club Malta:** Immerse yourself in the exciting environment of Havana Club Malta, a famous nightclub recognized for its electric energy and numerous music genres. Dance the night away to the newest sounds, have a cool beverage, and take up the energetic environment.

- **Gianpula Club:** Venture to the legendary Gianpula Club, a vast entertainment complex boasting various dance floors, pubs, and outdoor locations. Discover a range of music styles, from dance and techno to nostalgic hits and live performances.

- **Club Tropicana Malta:** Embrace the tropical ambiance of Club Tropicana Malta, a favorite venue for outdoor events and poolside celebrations. Enjoy live music, tasty beverages, and a calm environment amongst a tropical setting.

Explore the Diverse Entertainment Options Beyond Paceville

- **The Bridge Bar:** Discover the distinctive ambiance of The Bridge Bar, a modest place noted for its live music performances and intimate setting. Enjoy beautiful jazz sounds, taste a tasty meal, and relax in the company of friends.

- **The Black Pearl:** Immerse yourself in the real Maltese music culture at The Black Pearl, a classic Maltese band club. Experience the colorful environment, dance to traditional folk music, and experience the enthusiasm of local musicians.

- **St. James Cavalier:** Explore the unique mix of cultural activities at St. James Cavalier, a former British military hospital turned into a bustling arts center. Attend theatrical performances, art exhibits, and film screenings in a fascinating historical environment.

Venture Beyond the Tourist Hubs and Discover Local Gems

- **Fontana Jazz Club:** Venture to Fontana Jazz Club, a hidden treasure in Gozo, noted for its cozy setting and devotion to jazz music. Enjoy live performances by famous jazz performers, taste a glass of wine, and soak in the soulful vibrations.

- **Ta' Frenc Open-Air Cinema:** Experience the charm of open-air cinema at Ta' Frenc, a typical Maltese farmhouse surrounded by stunning scenery. Watch great flicks beneath the stars, have a picnic basket, and make wonderful memories.

- **Marsaxlokk Waterfront Bars:** Immerse yourself in the laid-back ambiance of Marsaxlokk's waterfront bars, a favorite area for residents to relax and enjoy the spectacular views. Savor a drink of local wine, dine on delicious seafood, and observe the colorful local life.

- **The tavern:** Explore The Pub, a typical Maltese tavern in St. Paul's Bay, recognized for its welcoming environment and unique local character. Savor a pint of local beer, have a delicious pub meal, and participate in discussions with friendly locals.

Tips for Enjoying Malta's Nightlife and Entertainment

- Plan your nights according to the opening hours of pubs, clubs, and entertainment venues.

- Dress accordingly for the sort of place you expect to visit.

- Be cognizant of local customs and traditions, and respect other patrons.

- Pace yourself and prevent overindulgence in drinks to guarantee a safe and pleasurable experience.

- Create treasured memories by shooting images and writing your nighttime adventures.

Embark on an exciting tour through Malta's nightlife and entertainment sector and explore a world of vivid energy, various music genres, and cultural encounters. From throbbing dance clubs to traditional music venues, Malta's nightlife gives an amazing experience that reflects the island's rich history and intense love for celebration.

Music and Festivals

Malta, provides a variety of music and festivals to satisfy all tastes and inclinations. From traditional Maltese folk music to worldwide pop singers, from quiet jazz clubs to large-scale open-air concerts, Malta's dynamic music scene offers a wonderful and engaging experience for visitors looking to immerse themselves in the island's culture and traditions.

Experience the Rhythm of Traditional Maltese Music

- **Festa Majjstral:** Immerse yourself in the colorful Festa Majjstral, held yearly in Mġarr, Gozo, a celebration of Gozo's patron saint, St. Peter and St. Paul. Discover traditional Maltese bands, enjoy folk music performances, and join in exciting processions and fireworks displays.

- **Malta International Folk Music Festival:** Discover the rich tradition of Maltese folk music at the Malta International Folk Music Festival, held yearly in different venues around the islands. Enjoy a range of traditional instruments, listen to heartfelt folk tunes, and observe the passion of local performers.

- **Notte Gozitana:** Experience the lovely Notte Gozitana, a festival held annually in Victoria, Gozo, displaying the island's distinct cultural history. Wander through neighborhoods decked with beautiful lights, listen to traditional Maltese folk music, and sample local specialties.

Embrace the Energy of Malta's Pop and Rock Festivals

Isle of MTV Malta: Immerse yourself in the electric atmosphere of Isle of MTV Malta, a famous music event hosted annually in Ta' Qali National Park. Discover worldwide pop and rock acts, dance to the newest sounds, and enjoy a dynamic environment among a varied audience.

- **Malta Music Week:** Experience the unique sounds of Malta Music Week, a series of performances and activities hosted yearly in various venues around the islands. Discover local and international musicians, enjoy a diversity of music genres, and see the inventiveness of Malta's music industry.

- **Earth Garden Festival:** Embrace sustainability and conscientious living at the Earth Garden Festival, held yearly at Ta' Qali National Park. Discover a variety of music styles, from electronic rhythms to traditional sounds, and engage in seminars on eco-friendly activities.

Venture Beyond the Main Festivals and Discover Hidden Gems

- **Fontana Jazz Club:** Venture to Fontana Jazz Club, a hidden treasure in Gozo, noted for its cosy setting and devotion to jazz music. Enjoy live performances by famous jazz performers, taste a glass of wine, and soak in the soulful vibrations.

- **St. James Cavalier Jazz Festival:** Immerse yourself in the world of jazz at the St. James Cavalier Jazz Festival, held yearly at Valletta's ancient St. James Cavalier Centre for Creativity. Discover worldwide jazz performers, enjoy live performances, and observe the enthusiasm for jazz among the local community.

- **Marsaxlokk Music Festival:** Experience the colorful Marsaxlokk Music Festival, held yearly in the lovely fishing hamlet of Marsaxlokk. Discover local bands and musicians, enjoy a range of music genres, and immerse yourself in the original Maltese environment.

Tips for Enjoying Malta's Music and Festivals

- Plan your festival itinerary in advance to guarantee you don't miss out on your favorite events.

- Purchase tickets or tokens in advance to avoid lengthy lineups and save time.

- Pace yourself and take pauses during the day to prevent exhaustion.

- Engage with local music fans and learn about the history and customs underlying the music.

- Create treasured memories by collecting images and writing your festival experiences.

Embark on a fascinating trip through Malta's music and festivals and experience a world of vivid rhythms, unique melodies, and cultural festivities. From traditional folk melodies to worldwide pop blockbusters, Malta's music industry gives a memorable experience that represents the island's rich past and strong love for music and entertainment.

Theater and Performing Arts

Malta, provides a plethora of theater and performing arts to satisfy all interests and inclinations. From traditional Maltese folk performances to worldwide ballet productions, from modest theater venues to huge opera halls, Malta's lively performing arts scene delivers a joyful and engaging experience for visitors looking to immerse themselves in the island's culture and traditions.

Experience the Magic of Traditional Maltese Theater

- **Teatru Manoel:** Step inside the ancient Teatru Manoel, Valletta's oldest theater dating back to 1732, and enjoy the beauty of traditional Maltese theater. Admire the exquisite architecture, see a compelling performance, and absorb up the rich cultural environment.

- **St. James Cavalier Centre for Creativity:** Immerse yourself in the numerous performing arts programs at St. James Cavalier Centre for Creativity, a former British military hospital turned into a thriving arts center. Discover modern dance performances, watch experimental theater shows, and experience the ingenuity of local artists.

- **MADC Theatre:** Venture to MADC Theatre, a famous venue for Maltese comedy and traditional folklore performances. Enjoy a night of comedy, immerse yourself in Maltese culture, and experience the passion of local performers.

Embrace the Grandeur of Opera and Classical Music

- **Mediterranean Conference Centre:** Experience the magnificence of opera at the Mediterranean Conference Centre, a contemporary theater noted for its world-class acoustics and big performances.

Attend a thrilling opera performance, enjoy a classical music event, and experience the brilliance of famous artists.

- **Manoel Theatre Opera Season:** Immerse yourself in the beautiful world of opera during the Manoel Theatre Opera Season, presented yearly at the ancient Teatru Manoel. Discover a selection of opera classics, relish the melodies of great composers, and experience the passion of opera performers.

- **Malta Philharmonic Orchestra:** Enjoy the lovely sounds of the Malta Philharmonic Symphony, a famous symphony noted for its enthralling performances. Attend a classical music performance, see the skill of local artists, and feel the beauty of symphonic music.

Venture Beyond the Main Venues and Discover Hidden Gems

- **Fort St. Elmo Open Air Theatre:** Experience the unique atmosphere of Fort St. Elmo Open Air Theatre, a historical fort renovated into an open-air theater. Enjoy a riveting drama beneath the stars, experience the merging of history and performance, and create lasting memories.

- **Theatrum Mobile:** Immerse yourself in the inventive works of Theatrum Mobile, a famous theater group recognized for its experimental and site-specific performances. Discover new theatrical experiences, observe the inventiveness of local artists, and deepen your knowledge of theater.

- **Festival Mediterranea:** Experience the lively Festival Mediterranea, held yearly in different places around the islands. Discover a broad spectrum of performing arts, from traditional Maltese dance to modern theatrical shows, and immerse yourself in the rich cultural history of the Mediterranean area.

Tips for Enjoying Malta's Theater and Performing Arts

- Plan your nights according to the performance schedules of theaters and venues.

- Dress properly for the sort of performance you intend to attend.

- Be cognizant of local customs and traditions, and respect other audience members.

- Turn off your cell phone and prevent distractions to completely immerse yourself in the performance.

- Create treasured memories by collecting images and writing about your theatrical and performing arts experiences.

Embark on a fascinating tour through Malta's theater and performing arts sector and experience a world of intriguing stories, charming tunes, and cultural expressions. From traditional Maltese folklore to world-class opera performances, Malta's performing arts give an outstanding experience that reflects the island's rich past and strong appreciation for creative expression.

Useful Malta Phrases

Greetings and Basic Expressions

- **Hello:** Bonġu (pronounced bon-joo)

- **Good morning:** Il-għodu t-tajjeb (pronounced eel-goo-doo taj-jeb)

- **Good afternoon:** Il-wara t-tajba (pronounced eel-war-ah taj-bah)

- **Good evening:** Is-serata t-tajba (pronounced ees-ser-ah-tah taj-bah)

- **Goodbye:** Sahha (pronounced sah-hah)

- **Please:** Jekk jogħġbok (pronounced yeck yaw-yowk)

- **Thank you:** Grazzi (pronounced gra-tsee)

- **You're welcome:** Merħba bik (pronounced mer-hba beek)

- **Excuse me:** Skuzi (pronounced skoo-zee)

Asking for Directions

- **Where is...?:** Fejn hi...? (pronounced fine hee...)

- **How do I get to...?:** Kif nasil biex immur...? (pronounced keef nah-sil be-yeks em-moor...)

- **Is it far?** Huwa 'l bogħod? (pronounced oo-wah bog-hod)

- **Can you show me on a map?** Tista' turihni fuq mappa? (pronounced tees-tah too-ree-ee fuq map-pah)

- **Straight ahead:** Dritta 'l quddiem (pronounced dree-ttah el goo-dee-em)

- **Turn left:** Dawwar xellug (pronounced dow-war shel-lugg)

- **Turn right:** Dawwar lemin (pronounced dow-war le-meen)

Asking Questions

- **How much does it cost?:** Kemm jiswa? (pronounced kemm yees-wah)

- **What is this in Maltese?** Kif tgħidha bil-Malti? (pronounced keef tee-dee-ha bil-mal-tee)

- **I don't understand:** Mhux nifhem (pronounced mix neef-em)

- **Do you speak English?** Titkellem bl-Ingliż? (pronounced tee-tel-lem beel-in-gleez)

- **Can you assist me?** Tista' tgħinni? (pronounced tees-tah tee-yee-nee)

Shopping and Dining

- **I would like...:** Nixti... (pronounced neek-stee...)

- **One:** Waħda (pronounced wah-dah)

- **Two:** Tnejn (pronounced tnyeen)

- **Three:** Tlieta (pronounced tlye-tah)

- **Four:** Erbgħa (pronounced er-bee-yah)

- **Five:** Ħamsa (pronounced ham-sah)

- **The bill, please:** Il-kont, jekk jogħġbok (pronounced eel-kont, yeck yaw-yowk)

- **This is extremely expensive:** Din għolja wisq (pronounced deen ghol-ya wisq)

- **I would prefer to pay via credit card:** Nixti nħallas bil-karta tal-kreditu (pronounced neek-stee nee-hal-las bil-kar-tah tal-kre-dee-too)

Additional Helpful Phrases

- **Yes:** Iva (pronounced ee-vah)

- **No:** Le (pronounced lee)

- **I need a doctor:** Ghandi bzonn tabib (pronounced gan-dee bzonn tah-beeb)

- I am lost: Intlift (pronounced int-lift)

- **Where is the bathroom?:** Fejn hi l-kamra tal-banju? (pronounced fine hee el-kam-rah tal-ban-yoo)

- **I am OK, thank you:** X'jismek? Jien tajjeb, grazzi (pronounced shee-yis-mek? yen tay-yeb, gra-tsee)

- **Enjoy your meal:** L-ikla t-tajba (pronounced lee-kla tay-bah)

- **Have a wonderful day:** Jum il-bierka (pronounced yoom il-beer-kah)

CONCLUSION

As your trip through the pages of this travel book draws to an end, we hope that you are filled with anticipation, excitement, and a greater knowledge of the lovely island of Malta. Whether you're planning a single trip, a romantic retreat, or a family holiday, Malta greets you with open arms and fascinating panoramas.

Malta, with its blue seas, ancient sites, and dynamic culture, provides a tapestry of experiences that will leave an unforgettable impact on your heart. From the busy districts of Valletta to the peaceful beauty of Gozo and Comino, the island calls you to explore its every corner.

Don't forget to taste the island's gastronomic wonders, from fresh fish collected in the Mediterranean Sea to the substantial flavors of traditional Maltese cuisine. Every meal in Malta is a celebration of island life and a voyage of flavor.

While Malta's beauty is evident, it is the warmth and kindness of its people that make it really distinctive. Engage with people, exchange smiles and pleasantries in Maltese, and you'll learn that Malta's heart is as hospitable as its surroundings are magnificent.

As you begin on your Maltese trip, don't forget to record the moments that steal your breath away. Let your camera and diary be your friends, recording the beauty, tastes, and feelings of this magnificent voyage.

Remember, a well-prepared journey is a more pleasurable one. From packing necessities to knowing local traditions, this book has provided you with the information you need to traverse Malta with confidence.

Malta is not simply a destination; it's a tale waiting to be told. It's a location where history whispers stories of ancient civilizations, where the Mediterranean Sea shimmers beneath the sun, and where every alleyway has the promise of discovery.

As you wave goodbye to Malta, know that the memories you've formed here will be with you forever. Whether you've visited hidden jewels, rested on sun-kissed beaches, or traveled through picturesque towns, Malta has left its stamp on your spirit.

While this tour may finish here, your adventure around Malta continues. May the memories you've acquired on this island be a source of pleasure and inspiration for years to come. And, when the time is perfect, may you come to Malta to create new tales, explore new frontiers, and revel in the timeless beauty of this Mediterranean treasure.

Malta is more than a destination; it's an invitation to explore, a canvas for your travels, and a location where every moment is a treasured memory. Until we meet again in this lovely corner of the globe, remember that the spirit of Malta is always with you, wherever your travels may take you next. Safe travels, and may your adventures be full of surprise and discovery, just as Malta has been for you. Saħħa! (Saħ-hah!) - Good health!

Printed in Great Britain
by Amazon